each one of us is a chapter

in the greatest story ever written ...

a narrative of exploration and discovery

remembered not only in myth

but encoded in our blood

every cell in our bodies

is charged with a miracle

that helps orchestrate

every pulse of sentient existence

Wade Davis, Ph.D,
Samuel Johnson winner, *Into the Silence*

EARLY ACCLAIM

"The teachings of Marlise Karlin's body of work give meaning to the most important sources of wisdom available to our world."
– **William A. Tiller** PhD. Professor Emeritus Stanford, Scientist, *What The Bleep Do We Know!?*

"Marlise's message has advanced decades in just the last three years. Her personal story validates her message. Absorb slowly with an open mind. Get ready for some mind-shifts."
– **Ron Willingham**, author, *Authenticity: The Head, Heart, and Soul of Selling*, former CEO, Integrity Systems Inc.

"Marlise is a fearless conduit for Divine love who has dedicated her life to providing individuals access to the greatest treasure of all."
– **Panache Desai**, named "A Contemporary Thought Leader" by Oprah Winfrey

"Marlise is a true explorer of 'inner space' who operates at the leading edge of consciousness. Her unique gifts in healing are seamlessly interwoven with electronic technology to create audio tapestries that exist in a class by themselves. Marlise walks her talk as she invites us on journeys of transformation and evolution."
– **Dr. Elliott Maynard**, Ph.D. Marine Sciences, Author *Brave New Mind,* Advisory Board, Research Integrity Institute

"Stillness Sessions became a constant companion wherever I traveled. I never grew tired of them, nor did I exhaust their potential ... which impressed me as being all the more powerful and profound, precisely because of their apparent yet deceptive simplicity."
– **Wade Davis**, Ph.D. Ethnobotanist, Samuel Johnson award-winning author of *Into the Silence*

"The Simplicity of Stillness has moved to a whole new level; with the science, and the audio technology Marlise developed, it's the most powerful healing tool I have ever experienced. I was also deeply moved by her work with ALS patients. I wish my fiancé could have experienced the SOS Method before he died. It would have made a huge difference for both of us."
– **Dr. Irene Conlan**, Former Assistant Director at the Arizona Department of Health Services

"Marlise's process of going into 'Stillness' is the most amazing I have experienced. I've listened 100 times and I love it because there is a freedom in every single moment."
– **Karen Elkins**, Editor and Founder of *Science to Sage Magazine*

"The Simplicity of Stillness program brings me to such a level of calm. I have been in pain since my early 20s, in excruciating pain because I have really bad fibromyalgia. And now it's gone. I have been feeling no pain in my body for over a year, which is a miracle in itself."
– **Robyn Rezny**, caregiver

"I was quite empty because of stress, lack of time, and worrying. Through The SOS Method I could connect myself within seconds, feeling amazing energy and complete happiness wherever I was."
– **Clemens Findeisen**, Faculty at International Centre for Development Studies

"I incorporate Stillness Sessions into my daily routine. It has helped me to stay calm, focused, and positive against a backcloth of adversity and uncertainty. It has helped me to evaluate and create some wonderful new possibilities."
– **Stephen Pauley**, CEO of Your Business Matters Ltd.

The
Simplicity
of Stillness®
method

marlise karlin

3 Steps to Rewire Your Brain, and Access Your Highest Potential

WATKINS

Sharing Wisdom Since
1893

This edition published in the UK and USA 2015 by
Watkins, an imprint of Watkins Media Limited
19 Cecil Court, London WC2N 4EZ

enquiries@watkinspublishing.co.uk

Edited by Dawn Bates
Typeset by Gina Carpenter
Graphic design by Cody Riise
Produced by Creative Plus Publishing Ltd.

The author of this book does not dispense medical advice or prescribe the
use of any technique as a form of treatment for physical, mental, or medical
problems without the advice of a physician, either directly or indirectly. The
intent of the author is only to offer information to assist you in your quest for
emotional and spiritual wellbeing. The author and the publisher assume no
responsibility for your actions.

A CIP record for this book is available from the British Library

ISBN: 978-1-78028-755-3

1 3 5 7 9 10 8 6 4 2

Printed and bound in China

The Simplicity of Stillness® and Stillness Sessions® are registered
trademarks of Inner Knowing International Inc., Inner Knowing International
Inc., 1539 W Sawtelle Blvd Ste 4, Los Angeles, California 90025

www.theSOSmethod.com

www.watkinspublishing.com

Also by Marlise Karlin

The Power of Peace in You

CONTENTS

FOREWORD

This book is groundbreaking – it combines cutting-edge science with ancient wisdom and, on top of this, the experiential tools required to access a state of consciousness that will facilitate transformation. Most books contain knowledge, however *The Simplicity of Stillness Method, 3 Steps to Rewire Your Brain & Access Your Highest Potential* provides both wisdom and the tools with which to effect real change.

We are now gaining an increasing awareness of our need to change belief systems, drop limiting fears and 'rewire' the brain/body, a requirement for true change in our lives. As both a physician and metaphysician of 30 years' experience, I constantly strive to help shift patients' reality from the helpless illness models in which they find themselves trapped – the cancers, depression, hereditary diseases or unhealthy relationships and soulless jobs. I aim to connect them to a world of *unlimited, infinite* healing possibilities for their lives as a whole. This is not easy with our natural skepticism and preconditioning. We need help to do this.

Marlise guides us through information and examples to elevate us to a new level, where we can change the old paradigms in our life with ease and grace. Using sound loaded with *information* in the *Stillness Session Technology* subtly impacts our vibrational frequency.

Many books talk about self-improvement, but *The Simplicity of Stillness Method* is the only one I've come across with scientifically researched audio tracks that shift your vibrational frequency into an actual state of stillness and peace. Years of research are present in this book –

interesting stories and examples of how working with these audio recordings in specific ways, and applying the 'tools' transformed people's lives in a remarkably short time.

My personal experience of listening to the Deep State Stillness Session recordings was an immediate feeling of peace. I noticed afterwards that subtle changes had come about: I was calmer, and also had lost some of my ingrained personality habits!

I am well acquainted with the concept of vibrational frequencies and the effect they can have. We are all subtly affected by frequencies in words, and music. Small changes result in large shifts, as can be seen from the many case studies. As Marlise says, "The more you connect to the healing power of unified Energy fields, the more your brain assists you by cycling new neural pathways."

This book leads you, easily, into connecting with the vital energy flows of the Universe: the ever-present light and the love. I invite you to experience for yourself how it can bring you into realms of stillness, peace, intuiting and healing on all levels.

Dr. Susan Jamieson, M. D.
An award-wining Scottish and Harvard educated physician, Dr. Susan Jamieson has been a specialist in integrative health for over 30 years. She combines the very best of Western and Eastern therapies, including traditional Chinese medicine and acupuncture. Known as the Light Doctor, she bridges science and mysticism to facilitate greater healing to her clients, who include some of the world's most famous rock stars – Lady Gaga, Coldplay, Elton John, The Black Eyed Peas, Mick Jagger and more.

PRELUDE

television station, Europe

Like so many who believe they are powerless, Sophie's lack of self-worth directed her roller coaster life. The night she discovered that patterns like these didn't have to formulate her future, a new sense of joy commingled with a rising passion to experience more. As days rolled into months the elements of *the method* she learned became the spine of strength and inspiration that ignited events beyond reason, events beyond what she ever dreamed.

Guided by truth, empathy and her newfound courage, the video Sophie made of the Russian President's upcoming visit to Austria revealed images of decadence juxtaposed with the violence of the Chechnya War. The Kremlin took notice, and when the television station she worked for refused to take it off the air, it created a noticeable domino effect in Putin's itinerary. Austrian national newspapers reported on the remarkable 20-second video that impacted a global leader's plans. Sophie smiled ... quietly ... not needing to tell anyone ... simply recognizing her true power as never before.

lakeside, upstate New York

The change was so unexpected and so subtle you might not even have noticed, except for the rose color in her cheeks, and how it got brighter and brighter as the Energy moved from my hands to hers and continued upward. The woman sitting on the steps of the historic mansion in upstate New York had come by 'chance' to accompany her friend to the program. She would soon discover how unfathomable this *coincidental* crossroad truly was and the remarkable impact it would have on her life.

Five days later when she returned, emanating vitality, it was clear her life had changed even before she spoke. She had completely stopped the nightly bouts of excessive wine-drinking and the antidepressant medication that had been her companion for the last 18 months. According to this radiant woman who couldn't stop sharing her good news with everyone, it happened without any withdrawals. Once the cloak of all that had suppressed her was removed, speaking up became natural – and this self-confessed timid individual became the exuberant person she truly was.

Maasai Mara, the plains of Kenya, Africa

"What is this?! It's an energy! Can you feel it too?! I do! WOW!!!" His ebony face lit up with excitement as awe and wonder replaced the habitual chatter of his mind, the dismal dialogue that often disturbs the unrealized promise within. Immersed in the moment, the whirlwind in his heart invited deeper introspection. "I have to sit down now ..."

On this night when the stars had lost their sparkle, hiding behind thunderous clouds, the moon smiled with a loving glance on Jackson, one of Africa's beloved Maasai. It was the beginning of an adventure that stemmed from the limitless potential activated as the Stillness Session began to play. The courage and optimism it ignited ultimately took Jackson around the world where he continued bringing hope into many people's lives.

Prelude

church hall, Atlanta, Georgia

Tears rolled down her face as she lifted her eyes to speak. The whispered words revealed a luminosity apparent only to those who have opened windowless portals in the night – that mystical joy Rumi eludes to in his poetry, which makes your heart yearn for the deep love expressed.

"I have never experienced this … in all the years I have wanted it, I have never known this …" Her tears continued to flow. As the invisible, energetic waves resonated through the words and music, she experienced the intrinsic and unimaginable connection she had always longed for. How could this happen, so unexpectedly in a room filled with people, seated in hard conference chairs, and on a night much like any other? Only it wasn't … How was this possible?

THE LONG & WINDING ROAD

the countless ups and downs ... of my life

When my father put his fist through the only locked door in the house to get at me, I knew I had no choice but to go. I didn't know where or how, but I climbed out my window that night to begin my search for true freedom. Not just from my father's abuse, but the anguish that can inscribe a lifetime of suffering on your heart.

Initially it led me down dark alleyways that included drugs and alcohol. When I became a single teen mom, it shifted my focus. I wanted to become responsible. It propelled my journey toward the study and research of what could give me deeper insight. I wanted to release the anger that was my constant companion, and find who I was beyond the definition my father had given me.

I spent years absorbing the teachings of masters, learning about ancient wisdom, and Eastern healing traditions,[1] not only intellectually but experientially as I spent time in their company. The mind-body research and application revealed how my mental and physical pain could heal, deepening my curiosity and study to include quantum science.

These choices guided and defined my professional success to become the International Director of a nonprofit Foundation where I traveled the world, and later an award-winning film producer. It was absolutely enjoyable, but I knew the happiness wouldn't last without attaining the internal freedom and love I still longed to know.

In 2001, an injury reignited my search. One day, seemingly out of the blue, my right hip began to hurt. I had done nothing physically to injure it, yet the symptoms got worse every day: excruciating pain, difficulty walking and sitting. Doctors were telling me I needed to consider back surgery.

When it's time, your soul's greatest longing is heard, whether you are conscious of it or not. For many people it arrives through the doorway of a challenge: a job loss, a death, an illness, or a major life crisis. Rarely do we consider these ordeals as messages ... but mine were speaking too loud to be ignored.

the only way out is by going deeper within

As the saying goes, you can run but you just can't hide. Well, I could barely walk, let alone run! At one point I yelled out in agony, *"I want to climb mountains in Peru ... I want to walk the deserts of Africa! What is it I need to know?!"* In the midst of unbearable pain, I realized the message sent was to remind me of my deepest longing – that I had somehow gotten lost along the way. I applied the tools I had personally synthesized from the various traditions I had studied – which now included setting a razor-like focus of Intention, with Making Requests (*see Tools, Teachings & Stories in Part 5*). I wanted answers, and by converging these tools with the potency of a Stillness meditation developed from the energetic healings I had received, the answers soon arrived.

I awoke one morning with a paralyzing sadness that seemed to penetrate every part of me. The thoughts crowding my mind sent spirals of incomprehensible shame and anxiety through my body. *How could I have done so many horrible things in my life?! I'll never know what true freedom is ... I'm not worthy ...* Everything I believed to be possible now seemed like a dream only a naïve mind could have conceived. The hopelessness I felt was overwhelming.

Tears flowed into uncaring pillows that couldn't comfort me. Nothing seemed to matter. It was all so meaningless. *How did I get here? Why was this happening?* The feelings surfacing weren't about my childhood difficulties. Instead, I watched as the screen of my mind displayed memories of the unconscious choices I had made during my life. Doing cocaine night after night. Drinking, drinking and more drinking. A visual screen of desolation streamed one shameful event after the next. *The freedom and love I longed to know was becoming an elusive dream again.* Here I was, seemingly at a lower rung of the ladder than I'd been for years. I felt so alone.

you don't even know ... what you don't know ... until ...

Suddenly, a stream of indefinable Energy began to course through me. Words can't describe the breathtaking sensations this form of liquid Love ignites, demonstrating an aliveness that brings our senses to new heights. All the negativity seemed to be drawn out of me, and as these thoughts and images were released, light began streaming into my vision. Sadness turned to wonder and awe. *It was beyond anything I ever believed possible. My perception of life was forever changed.* The experience continued for hours and then days and months as this illuminated knowing transmitted unexplainable events into my life.

I wondered if this experience would be a onetime occurrence, but they multiplied, and the energetic vitality flowing through me continued healing my mind and body.

The injury I had been suffering from turned out to be a gift as it actually spurred my practices to consistently connect with this healing power. Doctors had recommended back surgery when the pain had intensified to where I could no longer walk with ease, but within six months all the pain was gone, and it never returned. Access to this unified field of intelligence benefited every area of my life. Strengths appeared that inspired new decisions – fear and anxiety dissipated. My capacity for love seemed to overflow.

The teachings were experiential rather than conceptual. This energetic intelligence not only empowered my life, but everyone who came into contact with it – regardless of the form in which it was offered, whether through touch, sound, sight or intention. As more people evidenced the benefits that appeared in their lives through the simple processes I developed, I realized a new pathway was being set that I was meant to follow. I wrestled with the guidance that was leading me in a totally different direction than I ever imagined my life would take. But what happened when people connected with this healing power always moved me to tears – from releasing fear and depression to recognizing self-worth, from dissolving traumatic memories to igniting the inspiration that shifted global events. After seeing this, I knew there was no turning back.

the birth and evolution of
The Simplicity of Stillness

What I witnessed and experienced in the years to come inspired the development of *The Simplicity of Stillness Method (SOS)*. Synthesizing years of study with the latest scientific discoveries, I was able to develop a simple method that transmits the vital Energy force that healed my body and gave me access to an intelligence beyond what I had known.

My first book, *The Power of Peace in You*, presented the SOS method that brought remarkable benefits into many people's lives around the globe, which included practical tools to bring it into everyday. *The Simplicity of Stillness Method, 3 Steps to Rewire Your Brain, & Access Your Highest Potential* is the evolution of that process.

I've included landmark scientific research along with the SOS Tools, Teachings and Technology to assist you in choosing the best direction for you at each turn in your life, along with the stories and case studies of people who reveal the wonder of what's possible for each of us today. You'll discover that releasing patterns, increasing vitality, getting healthy and finding inspiration each day is not only do-able – it's simpler than you think.

Whether you have been on a track of higher learning for years, or have just decided to head out on a voyage of new discovery, *The Simplicity of Stillness* gives you an ability to live in the flow of life where this exquisite intelligence brings more joy into each day, and where you access the 'sweet spot' of life we all want to live in. As the saying goes, 'life is either a daring adventure or nothing' – and when you live connected to this evolutionary power, it always is the former. I'm ready, are you?

With Great Love,

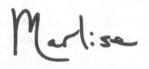

JUST FOR YOU
STILLNESS SESSION TECHNOLOGY

Stillness Sessions are newly developed technology that transmits a vital life energy on carrier waves of sound. These scientifically researched audio recordings of beautiful music and words activate deep peace and the flow of higher awareness.

www.theSOSmethod.com/sos3audios

SCAN QR CODE TO PLAY AUDIO
Special Tip: For ease of access put your Stillness Sessions on your cell phone, ipad/kindle, & computer. For listening pleasure use headphones.

To access this material you will need to enter the following code when you reach the page. Code: U2KOE1LS

Deep State Stillness

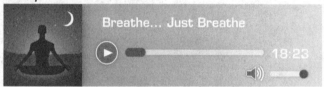

Breathe... Just Breathe

18:23

Sacred Word Session

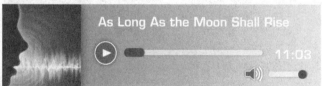

As Long As the Moon Shall Rise

11:03

Elevate Session

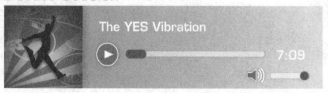

The YES Vibration

7:09

If you would prefer to receive your Stillness Sessions on a CD, simply visit the website above and select the "get a CD" option.

walls of illusion fall

as the blueprints of your past that created them

rise from the depths of an unconscious sea

one by one they dissolve … the game is finally over

golden notes of clarity reveal

the power in pure love

honor that … and when you do …

your life will become a reflection

of the shimmering light

that lives in you

Marlise Karlin

PART 1
SIMPLE ACCESS FOR
A MODERN WORLD

ACTIVATING YOUR
HIGHEST POTENTIAL
living in the flow of life

What if you could feel more joy, release what worries you, become highly intuitive and have a healthier body – simply by putting on headphones and hitting 'play'?

This might seem like a totally improbable question. I wouldn't have believed it was possible 14 years ago myself, but what I have witnessed and what you will read in this book reveals potential beyond the boundaries of what we've been taught. It's easy to see how technological changes in the last few years are bringing a uniquely different world into existence; all you have to do is look around you, in every area of life. Now, we can use these advances to assist us in the most beneficial ways imaginable.

We can accelerate our intelligence, and develop better health, habits and behavior – more rapidly than we ever envisioned. The promise of this book is to show you how that is possible *experientially* through a method that matches the way we live today, bringing together the most time-honored teachings, and recent scientific discoveries, implemented with instruments of modern life, from cell phones to computers to media systems.

What I want to share with you upfront is that making something simple and direct – hasn't been all that simple! The process was always powerful; the challenge was to make it simple. The Simplicity of Stillness Method has been *road tested* for almost 14 years, and has demonstrated the most phenomenal benefits in thousands of people's lives and in my own. The timing has now brought it all together, where profound and practical, powerful and simple, ancient and modern have been realized. So, let's look at how this all came about.

frustration can be a great instigator

I spent years feeling frustrated, thinking of To Do lists while attempting to connect with that place of peace and clarity meditation can offer. I believe many people encounter similar frustrations – otherwise why wouldn't masses of people practice it?! Who wouldn't want an ability to cope with stressful situations, have more joy, connection with others, and the many benefits touted?

Meditation is a practice that has benefitted humanity since the first breath was taken on an inward journey – and yet, for the majority of people alive today, it's not even on their radar. "There's just not enough time," "It doesn't work for me," "It's boring," "My mind thinks too much." These are all great reasons why universal intelligence must have decided to deliver new tools and technology for connecting to that transcendent flow of life.

new technology to match this time

The Simplicity of Stillness Method defines new points of entry for activating your highest potential. The heart of this method is the Stillness Sessions audio technology which can be practiced in the middle of a busy life by "simply putting on headphones and hitting play." It's a scientifically researched technology to bring higher consciousness into your life without even having to close your eyes, spend 20 minutes, or find a quiet space.

And, it isn't about giving up that exquisite space of meditation, as Stillness Sessions accelerate your experiences of deep meditation and the benefits that provides. They have also evidenced mind-body healing and the potential that develops the biochemistry to calm *and/or* vitalize you. This dynamic and more will be explained in depth in the upcoming chapters. One remarkable distinction of the Stillness Sessions Technology is that:

YOUR MIND DOESN'T HAVE TO BECOME STILL FOR IT TO WORK

When I observed this happening, it broke through a lifetime of conventional knowledge I had entrusted as 'truth'. Entrenched beliefs of all kinds, especially those passed down for centuries, are not easy to break! And the dissolution of this one made me so happy! For all of you who have struggled with meditation, you can now breathe a sigh of relief. You can have direct access to that highly beneficial state of inner awareness normally achieved through years of meditative practice, and, in a form you could love. After all, who doesn't like listening to music? Long-time meditators will also love what this next-generation technology offers, as this stream of accelerated intelligence will always boost your inward journey, and can be added to your existing practice.

Another element of SOS you will enjoy is the 'proof' of your connection, which can be recognized in various ways, including physical 'tingling' sensations throughout the body, heat, cold, and many more indicators that alleviate that "did anything happen?" doubt many have with meditation. I have countless emails from people whose practice includes Stillness Sessions, and they talk about how *totally* different this experience is from any meditation they have ever done – and that I really should find a new name for it. How do you express in words these experiences (you will read about in the stories) where there isn't a relatable definition other than the one we all know? I have yet to find an answer.

The more practiced you become at going about daily activities from the higher frequency it ignites, the more you'll reflect the love, joy, inspiration and creativity that stem from being in this natural and yet uniquely different *experiential flow of life*. As you tap into this heightened potential, you'll notice how swiftly your life circumstances mirror the wellbeing you have begun to resonate.

YOUR HIGHEST POTENTIAL = LIVING IN A PROFOUND FLOW OF LIFE

Accessing infinite intelligence develops your ability to live from your highest potential. The healing it offers releases anxiety and fear, and develops behavioral change where loving relationships, prosperity and purpose inspire your life each day.

Living at your highest potential is not about climbing a ladder of success defined by an unconscious ego-driven mindset. It's about discovering a flow of life that is so rewarding it feeds your mind, body and soul. You have the security of knowing that wherever you put your focus, whether it is on your health, mental, emotional or spiritual wellbeing, insight beyond learned 'thinking' will *always* be there.

Why have people forgotten the relevance of connecting with this innate power?

- The overwhelming challenges in every day
- The inability to find and experience peace
- The limitations of conventional mind chatter
- The belief of powerlessness to break negative patterns

When we are under everyday or critical stress from crisis, disappointment, loss or sudden illness, our bodies react by flooding our nervous systems with chemicals. It becomes harder to think clearly or function at our best, and easy to believe you are powerless to break negative patterns.[1]

dangers of the linear mind

When you are going about your day operating from the linear mind, you only have access to a fraction of the truth and wisdom that is available to you. It's like going through life with blinders on. Life is infinitely harder and more stressful. Since we are exceedingly more skilled and practiced in having our perceptions and decisions rooted in our minds, our lives are often expressions of the frenetic whims and fluctuations of that conditional state.

When you are connected to that energetic stream of life, it carries you effortlessly over the threshold where the limited linear mind ends and that vast well of infinite intelligence begins. Your mind becomes curious to seek the information that exists beyond the education we've been given. SOS provides an effortless method of transporting your consciousness to that inner well of limitless wisdom. The mind's purpose will become even better defined in later chapters through newly discovered science that evidences just how powerful it can be.

Why include The Simplicity of Stillness in your life?
 • To access deep peace and your highest potential in a simple, experiential and effective way
 • To consistently connect to inspired solutions and actions
 • To heal your mind and body from recent and past suffering
 • To influence your brain physiology and neurotransmitters
 • To release blockages in the cellular structure of the body

When you apply any of the SOS Tools (*see Part 5*), you are putting focus on a specific area. By activating that focus with the Energy potential in Stillness Sessions, it heightens your ability to find solutions, and answers. You experience being in a *flow of life*, accompanied by feelings of pleasure and happiness.

Exploration of this evolutionary way of learning is through:

- **Expansion of the advanced life Energy** that consistently expands, and heals your mental, emotional and physical wellbeing.

- **Evidence of the benefits** in your own life, i.e. there is nothing you have to believe. When you see it happening, you know.

- **Activating your brain's neurotransmitters** to develop new patterns that realign you with the ever-present 'flow of life'.

- **Harmonizing energy fields** within the body that purify stagnation from stress.

To get in this *flow*, it is essential to incorporate the rocket fuel that supplies this super boost and the tools that bring it into every day. By applying the tools, teachings and technology in this book, a person's entire life trajectory can shift into an emerging mastery. Living connected to your highest potential is a treasure we are all here to know.

NEW AVENUES TO
SUPER-AWARENESS
evolutionary tools for today

Have you noticed how everything seems to have speeded up? The digital revolution has given us so many innovative elements for living, but has it also made life more difficult? Society's new norm states that faster is better and so people are constantly rushing around, trying to meet this model of success. Kids as well as adults feel overwhelmed on a daily basis.

Fuelled by anxiety, the only way to ease the pressure seems to be through pleasurable activities that release stress. Ultimately it develops the *more* syndrome ... and usually it's not more of what brings long-lasting benefits and joy, but more retail therapy, alcohol, drugs, sex and video games for those inclined. This cycle of momentary relief dissipates swiftly as it can't liberate the cravings to fill the emptiness inside.

That was last week.

This week, those circumstances don't affect you in the way they did before. Imagine, for a moment, being in the midst of a challenging day, and yet you are in a place of clarity magnified by an immense vital power and inner stillness. You have a centered connection. You know where solutions to life's challenges exist and how to get them. This *knowing* enlightens your daily decisions, and inspires a way of being that is resilient, intuitive, creative and caring. Your life has begun to reflect the vitality that streams through every part of your mind and body.

Is this possible?

It is when you access a 'super-awareness' – the source of advanced life Energy. The Simplicity of Stillness simplifies the complexities of life as it advances your connection to this higher intelligence that is your true birthright. As this advanced life Energy expands, heightened creativity, courage and love naturally inspire your actions. A new enthusiasm for life appears.

In the *Prelude* each person discovered the remarkable possibilities of what can happen when this Energy is activated. This is the evolution of what is available for each of us today.

By converging Eastern wisdom and healing traditions, The New Science, and over a decade of case studies – practical and effective processes that activate neurotransmitters in the brain, energy flows in the body and *super-awareness* were developed. Using the energetically enhanced Stillness Sessions audio technology and the SOS Tools included here, the quality of people's lives improved, as well as the healing of physical impairments.

how belief systems block our reasoning

So what could bring about the life-altering changes these people evidenced? What we know today is that the brain contains the physical embodiment of our knowledge, emotions, memories, beliefs, personality and character. According to centuries-old doctrine, it wasn't reasonable to assume that the human brain could change in any significant way – especially one that would support transformative shifts of this magnitude. I preface 'today' – as things are changing so swiftly that what is assumed to be a 'fact' in this moment can easily become tomorrow's dogma. These doctrines had to be amended when research reported new documentation of the brain's plasticity, meaning the brain *can* change!

Years of entrenched beliefs have recently eroded in many areas of science that impact our entire lives. In *Part 3, The New Science* it demonstrates specifically where this is true. One important doctrine that has dissolved is that we now know that new pathways can be formed in the brain that affect behavioral change.' And, yet, what occurred for some of the people in the *Prelude* was so rapid, it would seem there wasn't even time to form a 'new pathway'. Could the *energetic field* Albert Einstein referred to in his renowned quote, "The field is the sole governing agency of the particle" shine a light on these occurrences?

If the field is energy and particle is matter, and physics says that the field is what shapes matter ... then was it *this intelligent Energy* that *shaped* the realignment of life and perception in these people and in me? Was it like the alchemy of how a rock can become crystal, only speeded up? How carbon can become a diamond? Did it also have the power to orient neural pathways to continually shift life's compass? If so, how often would you need to bring this directional experience into your life to see a metamorphosis this extensive?

It's difficult to grasp the importance of emerging ideas and how they can apply to our own life when they appear as fragments of information in the midst of a busy day. By bringing together The New Science that explains what is now possible, with case studies that evidence it, and a method to bring it into your life, you can begin to more fully recognize *your* capabilities. As we all know, if you don't believe it's possible – it won't be for you. Maybe we can finally release the sense of powerlessness ingrained in each of us and recognize greater potential than what we have known.

WHAT'S IN THIS BOOK

This book's purpose is to offer you an ability to create, heal and inspire – your life as well, as others. The SOS method; the Tools, Teachings and Technology have the power to transform self-defeating patterns and to assist you in living from your highest potential. How this is possible and how you can bring this knowledge and experience into your life you will discover through the following:

- **The Simplicity of Stillness Method** outlines the essential elements that bring long-lasting benefits into your life in 3 Simple Steps – Apply, Activate, Act.

- **The New Science** clarifies what is relevant to understand regarding limiting beliefs and reveals landmark discoveries that define what is possible today.

- **Stillness Sessions Technology** fuels this method. It is scientifically researched sound recordings of music and words that transmit advanced life Energy, offered in three uniquely different formats included with this book (*see Just For You Stillness Sessions*).

- **SOS Tools & Teachings** offer knowledge that enhances the mind's capabilities and the directed focus tools that establish new conscious habits.

- **Stories & Case Studies** support the development of new beliefs of your limitless potential, and show what occurs when you connect with advanced Energy potential, release blocked cellular memory in your body, and imprint new neural pathways.

- **Questions, Insights & Reflections** stimulate reflection on the phenomena, the wonder, the challenges and the hope – the elimination of negative patterns, and the actualization of new abilities and self-healing.

the evolution of SOS

When my publisher asked me to write a second edition of *The Power of Peace in You*, I agreed, but so much had evolved that I literally found it impossible to do. Evolution is just that – constant change. While you always want to incorporate the wisdom you have attained, you don't want to stop your evolutionary process. Once I began writing this book, even more information began pouring in from that field of all intelligence, resulting in what I believe will take your life journey to the next level, as it did mine.

There are favorite stories I was asked to include and many new ones from the scientific study on SOS that I believe will assist you in recognizing the phenomenal capabilities available to each of us today when we connect with this super-awareness. Whatever you do, I suggest you don't put the book down until you have read *The Universe's Big Mistake*, *The Relentless Pain of Being a Hero*, and *Step Over That Line (see Part 5)* – as they are the kind of stories you can read over and over. Some include word-for-word transcripts that give you a view into the world of phenomenal healing and empowerment, and exactly how it occurs.

Whether you are looking for experiences of inner peace rarely known, consistent access to your creative potential, relaxation, or to connect with worlds beyond this reality – it's possible. You are the one guiding the journey through the choices you make and how you apply this method in your life.

You will find answers to what you are looking for and even some that you might not have begun to question. The intelligence that inspired this book continues to evolve our access to the many gifts it has to offer. All those reasons about not having enough time can now dissipate in the embers of illusion that want to separate you from your true power.

HOW TO READ THIS BOOK

I invite you to read this book in its entirety, as it unfolds the mystery and the reality of how rapidly we can evolve. There are new frontiers to more deeply understand which are included in The New Science and Subtle Energies sections of the book. Each chapter offers you information that reshapes unconscious beliefs of powerlessness and activates conscious ways of BE-ing (habits and behavior) that inspire every part of your life. How To Use This book (*see opposite*) informs how you can begin to incorporate the benefits from day one.

This book can enlighten and support anyone's journey, of any age and culture, as the SOS method is practiced today by people of all ages and walks of life. There is no one way to evolve, and, if your life is not reflecting what you find happening in the stories here, then I hope with all my heart that you will give this method a try as the gifts it offers reveal how truly amazing you are.

HOW TO USE THIS BOOK

Stillness Sessions Technology: My suggestion is to begin by listening to the Stillness Session recordings right away; as this is the dynamic element that ignites peace, higher awareness, and many benefits (instructions are in *Part 4, Stillness Sessions*). You can listen to one or two a day as some are only 7 minutes in length. These audio recordings impact your life from the first time you listen to them.

SOS Teachings: The Teachings offer knowledge from ancient wisdom, healing traditions and science. The stories and case studies evidence what is possible for each of us when we connect to this dynamic experience and bring it into the everyday of our lives. As you reflect on this knowledge, it can assist in diminishing self-defeating beliefs and establishing new ones that empower you.

SOS Tools: accelerate your ability to directly focus on what you want to create, release, intend or develop in your life. You can apply each SOS Tool as you read the chapter *or*, after you have fully absorbed all the information in the book, you can return to the Tool that seems most relevant in your life at the moment. It's important to include all three elements to receive the best results possible, and if you prefer there is also a 21 day plan that outlines a simple way to do this (*see Staying Connected*). If you want to feel good, enjoy life and share what truly brings meaning to every day, this simple method can powerfully light the way.

ANCIENT ART &
THE NEW SCIENCE
igniting an unprecedented future

My father always stated his opinions, loud and clear. Sarcasm and cynicism mixed with a southern drawl, as though that would make them more palatable. This time his tone was threatening, "Damn it Marlise, you just don't know how to listen, do you?! That's not medicine, it's like voodoo! I'm going to call down there and report those people!"

I had discovered an ancient art of healing that brought answers to questions I hadn't even known to ask, and for some reason this seemed threatening to my father's beliefs. I was diagnosed in my 20s with PID, pelvic inflammatory disease; the doctors suggested it could possibly be from the faulty birth control devices implanted in those days. The symptoms would be resolved for a time from heavy doses of antibiotics, but then the illness would come back again full force. My doctors agreed a hysterectomy was the only possible cure. The pain was immense but that wasn't the route I wanted to take. I needed to find a new solution and soon, as continuous bouts of this illness were devastating my life.

I was willing to try anything. A friend recommended Jin Shin Jyutsu (JSJ), an ancient art of healing that works on energy pathways in the body.[1] Within a year of having treatments my symptoms completely vanished – no drugs, no hysterectomy. I later discovered through my doctor that the treatments had even cleared the internal scarring they expected to find. This 'voodoo' my father was concerned about had healed me.

In many ways, his opinions were understandable; they reflected the beliefs so many still have – that chronic illnesses can only be cured through surgery and drugs.

clearing out the cobwebs

When my mother was diagnosed with cancer of the lip a few years later, she asked if she could join me in Arizona, where I continued with my personal *stay healthy* plan twice a year. I guess the concern about her illness registered louder than my father's warnings. My mother's first treatment was with Mary Burmeister, a tiny Japanese lady who was a master teacher in her own right, having studied with the founder for over 30 years.[2] I was excited to hear my mother's response after her session, as treatments with Mary always made me feel like the earth had moved.

She replied in an offhand manner, "It was a lovely little massage." I was stunned. My mother didn't seem to get it – at all! This really worried me. For one, Jin Shin Jyutsu isn't anything like a massage. Did that mean it wouldn't work because she didn't *understand* it? How energy in the body that becomes blocked through negative patterns and stresses can be released. Mary had instructed and shared with me many idioms of the mind-body relationship, and how what you think and say can influence the internal messages that develop illness – if my mother didn't understand this, would the treatments work?

Mary's response was classic, it's one that has guided me for years: *"Must one know that their house is being cleaned? Or will they notice the difference once it has been done?"* Everyone *gets it* on the level they can. As long as they are open to the art of healing, understanding will grow as limitations are released – in the body as well as in the mind.

making friends with the unknown

A few weeks after my mother returned home, I called to see how she was doing. She chatted about this and that, and then in a very offhand manner stated that the doctors had told her the cancer was gone.

"What?! Really?" Now I was amazed. I asked my mother what other treatments she tried. She said the doctors had given her an ointment to apply, which she used for a week. It had never cured anyone, but they felt it was worth a try. When the doctors ran tests on my mother after she returned, they were astounded. There wasn't a trace of her cancer left. They even told her they thought it couldn't be from the ointment as it had never brought results like this.

The house had been cleaned. It was noticed. While my mother might not have understood what contributed to her overall wellness – *she was open* and she did the treatments. She continued to stay open and to learn about what she now realized that she didn't fully comprehend – the correlation between illness and her mind and body. We spoke about how she would try to release the anger she had about Daddy's drinking by yelling at him over the years, and how little it affected him, but was emotionally difficult for her.

Although the lip cancer never returned, years later my mother was diagnosed with Hepatitis C, a disease that attacks the liver. How interesting that my Dad, the alcoholic, had no problems with his liver, and the one who was angry, my mother

– did. My mother continued 'cleaning house' for the rest of her life, enjoying the peaceful feelings she got during her Jin Shin Jyutsu treatments and later when I developed SOS, she listened to Stillness Sessions and had the direct healing treatments I offered her to shift old patterns of anger as well. She lived more than 15 years past the doctor's diagnosis.

This journey of life continually uncovers hidden mysteries. What I discovered through case studies and the Scientific Study on The Simplicity of Stillness validated knowledge I had learned from the healing traditions of old. The New Science added elements that defined where the emotional states that distress our systems could come from – and the new discoveries offered understanding of the phenomena occurring in the world today, and what is still to come. Before we get to the science, I want to define the difference between 'healing' and a 'cure' as it relates to The Simplicity of Stillness.

healings and cures

Healings occur in many forms; mental, emotional and spiritual, as well as physical. For an illness to be 'cured', the associated physical symptoms usually disappear. A physical cure can be dramatically evidential – while a mental and emotional 'healing' might not be – but it can have a long-lasting effect on a person's life that is also dramatically evidential.

'Healing' is not a specific result-oriented focus. It is not about the *absence* of illness – as much as it's about the *presence* of higher awareness. It's about being in harmony with the flow of life, discovering what universal intelligence has designed specifically for your evolutionary journey. It's an opening into wellbeing beyond the traditional definition. Symptoms of the illness may or may not still be there, but the person feels at peace. They could suddenly be inspired to be in the world in an entirely different way.

A person who has a chronic illness could be cured of it, but it might not affect the anger and regret from a past incident that continues to cause ongoing distress, which could possibly lead to regression or future illness.

Imagine an unprecedented future that includes the best of modern medicine with methods that reconnect you to your innate power, to generate self-healing in all areas of your life. Imagine how great that will be.

There are many forms of healing that occur for people when they access higher Energy fields. You will read about some of these unusual occurrences in later chapters. Some of the healings that happened when people began applying The Simplicity of Stillness processes occurred rapidly, and others over time; the benefits tend to be life long. Rather than what people think *should* happen, people discover what has been designed specifically for their journey. To understand where we've been, and where we're headed, let's look more deeply into the latest discoveries that can enlighten the road ahead.

converging the old with the new

This is where ancient wisdom, the healing arts and science converge to paint a picture that will assist you in having greater compassion for yourself and others – and the insight of what is needed to accelerate more joy and strength in every day. If you believe you are powerless, it will have an obvious effect. *It isn't what you intellectually know that influences your health and wellbeing – it's what you unconsciously believe and practice.*

the new science

The New Science of Epigenetics, DNA, Neuroplasticity and Subtle Energies are specific areas of science that play an important role in your life. As you add information to your library of acceptance, this knowledge can more readily support the development of beliefs and habits that increases your sense of confidence, clarity and worthiness.

The dynamic of the SOS method assists you by unifying experience with knowledge and action. I will be weaving these specific elements throughout the book. Can independent scientific discoveries, when brought together, culminate in a broader understanding of the power we each have to *clean house*? Can we recognize our potential in new ways that were previously blocked by dogma unwittingly passed on to us as 'facts' and 'truth'? Seeing these elements side by side can cultivate exponential growth and understanding.

I invite you to allow the information to inform, inspire and reveal the impact that unconscious and/or empowering beliefs have in our lives. Much of what this emerging science demonstrated put a footnote or exclamation mark on what I learned through previous studies of healing traditions. It made me wonder, what other doctrines are in place that it's time to break through?

There is so much beyond what has been proven by conventional standards that can bring about wellbeing today. There are scientists, as well as those in the healing arts, that are out on the leading edge making discoveries that will impact every part of our lives. It's not easy for new discoveries to break through the intellectual prejudice that has often shunted the stunning powers of our true capabilities. As this knowledge comes to light, it will dramatically impact our future.

I had a remarkable conversation with Bruce Lipton, an internationally recognized developmental biologist, and bestselling author of *The Biology of Belief*, on the difficulties many scientists face, "The whole understanding," he explained, "comes down to a very interesting difference between the conventional world of science and the new science that's unfolding – *the new science is dealing with vibration, and fields, and energy* ... and we've left that out of the equation in our conventional world because conventional biomedicine doesn't entertain the influence of 'the field', which in physics says, 'My God, that's the one that shapes the matter ... and we've ignored it'."[3]

breaking down unquestioned doctrines

It seems that history is continually being repeated. When scientific reports surface that don't fit previous established norms, they are either ignored or claimed to be false. A Hungarian doctor Ignaz Semmelweis had a theory for disinfection in 1846 and was ridiculed for his unconventional ideas. At the time, doctors passed diseases from one patient to the next because they didn't realize the connection between germs and contagious disease. They didn't know infection could spread as they went from patient to patient without washing and disinfecting their hands. Semmelweis was considered a radical upstart, and his work was only recognized to be important after his death. Now, as we know, his breakthrough findings are common practice throughout the world. What can we learn from this?

Not every theory will ultimately become recognized as fact or truth, but I believe it's important to look at all the information as it becomes available with an open mind, and then, by tapping into your experiential wisdom, *you* can make the important decisions in your life accordingly.

21st-century innovation

When you are ill, you suddenly become much more open to new ideas. I credit the illnesses and injuries in my life as instrumental crossroads that guided me into the now 20+-year education of what infuses The Simplicity of Stillness with the knowledge it offers.

I invite you to be open and allow your natural curiosity to uncover what heightens your ability to mine the gold fields of your innate potential, health and wellbeing. The science, ancient teachings and often inexplicable events you'll read about here can become an effective mirror for learning.

Research has shown us there are mirror neurons in the brain that, once activated, can assist in rapid and somewhat unconventional ways of learning – where what you *observe* is as effectively integrated as what you actually practice or *do*. Imagine the ease and simplicity this could offer your mind.

This exploration into new discoveries offers insights and advantages that would be difficult to get without linking these important elements:

• *Could the science introduced in the following chapters increase your ability to be healthier and to bring elegant solutions to whatever challenges you?*

• *Could it unlock beliefs that have stopped you from living at your highest potential?*

To further unravel this compelling information that has been locked away for lifetimes – that is, until now – all you have to do is stay open ... and establish a new pattern for 'cleaning house' that consistently clears out the dust ... so you can live in an unprecedented future ... enjoying the adventure that life truly is.

ENERGY & AWARENESS
exploring subtle energies

When the mind wants to fully understand new information, it often wrestles with it instead of allowing it to be absorbed. I was learning about the energetic flows in the body from Mary who, as I mentioned earlier, was a master teacher of the healing arts. Each time a flurry of hands would be raised with questions – her initial and, on reflection, incredibly simple and insightful response was, *"Just smile ... drop your shoulders ... and breathe ..."*. She would always try to calm the person's mind as the first step, and once they were reassured that there *were* answers, she would continue to clarify *experientially* what her words were trying to express intellectually.

When the mind can grasp what is possible, it supports the adventure of our evolutionary journey. And when you invite deeper understanding from the highest knowledge – answers will always appear to deepen the wisdom given. I have redefined a few words to set this in motion. Let's begin with Awareness and then move into new definitions for Energy that are redefining the future *today*:

AWARENESS
- **Awareness (capital 'A') is a profound experiential state of inner connection where there is no worry, fear, anger, or suffering**. It is a depth of peace, accessed through Energetic intelligence that has the power to rewire patterns in the mind and body to free you. Not in some distant future. Now.

- **awareness (lowercase 'a') is a practice to become more present; to become mindful,** to observe when you act from an emotional or chemical trigger – and to choose a new direction.

Without accessing the Awarenesses described above, you might think, as I did, that the package you came in with – your intelligence, your genes, your predisposition to being unhappy or feeling unworthy – is just the way it is – defining what you get in this lifetime. And sure, you can study and dedicate yourself to getting out of that box, *but there is only so far you can go* ... Could this be another outdated belief system? It is certainly no longer a fact.

What I discovered through that life-altering energetic experience and those that arrived later, redefined my perception of what is possible beyond this mindset. Even 20 years of study paled in comparison to the Awareness I experienced in those timeless events. What began to occur in my life, in the days and months to follow, synthesized a currency of information that continues to advance new insight today.

ENERGY

Energy is not just an abstract conceptual theory, it is something that affects our lives that can be worked with and experienced. Albert Einstein researched the quantum sea and established that it connects every living entity. The apparent separation between us is more accurately evidence of something unseen, and that *something unseen* is Energy.

Five fundamental principles of energy

1. Everything in the universe consists of energy – human beings are energy in form.
2. Human beings vibrate at different frequencies dependent on their level of mental, emotional, physical and spiritual coherence.
3. Various energy(ies) comprise this universe; dense energies, as well as subtle energies of higher intelligence.
4. The Energy field of consciousness, light and peace is a high vibration that can reconstruct disharmony and density within the mind and body naturally over time
5. This unified field that sustains and maintains our world is given different names depending on your personal preference; God, Buddha, nature in its evolution, the quantum sea, Source.

DENSE ENERGIES

We know about the physical fields; modern physics has taught us about four well-known forces of energy; electrical, magnetic, thermal and gravitational. They are often referred to as 'dense energies'. Each of these forces can be measured using conventionally recognized scientific instruments.

We are surrounded and often feel bombarded by dense energy – from the electromagnetic (EM) waves that power our media and technological systems, to people sending out unconscious negativity, and from various other frequencies that drain and exhaust our innate abilities. Research has recently shown that what is being transmitted from these dense electromagnetic waves could possibly lead to various disorders – memory disruption, insomnia, hormonal imbalances, and cancer. Connecting with a higher energetic flow that harmonizes, nurtures, and fosters wellbeing in you, is an essential element to combat this influence.

SUBTLE ENERGIES

A new generation of quantum physicists believes that the secrets of the energy-matter bond in the universe can be understood only by considering the invisible dimensions of 'subtle energies' (SE). Subtle energies (complex frequencies) broadcast *beyond* the four accepted classes, meaning they cannot be explained by the known principles of the electromagnetic (EM) field of matter/energy. Our knowledge with regard to subtle energies is only just beginning as it contributes to phenomena not currently explained by conventional science. These occurrences have tangible effects that can be and are documented (see research below and case studies throughout the book).

'SUBTLE ENERGIES' ARE A MEDIUM THROUGH WHICH CONSCIOUSNESS ACTS ON THE REALM OF MATTER AND ENERGY

Subtle energies are resonance-vibrations of the unified field that pioneering scientists have redefined in the last century. Dr. William A. Tiller, Professor Emeritus at Stanford University, is among a roster of courageous scientists who stepped outside the boundaries of conventional science to follow the inner direction that inspired his research in this area. For over 40 years he collected data and did various studies on subtle energies, intentionality and consciousness. In *Science and Human Transformation*, Dr. Tiller documents groundbreaking research that significantly affected the properties of material and physical reality through intention and its effect on lowering and raising the pH of water (by 1 unit.) Another way to understand this is like changing salt water into pure water.[1]

According to Dr. Tiller, "When you get to the acupuncture meridian system, you're going beyond electromagnetics. You're starting to get into the subtle energy domains." Eastern philosophies revealed this wisdom, regarded as eternal, in ancient records written before the birth of Buddha.[2] Healing traditions such as acupuncture and Jin Shin Jyutsu,[3] can go beyond the electromagnetic waves humans generally emit, allowing subtle energies to flow through meridians, energetic pathways in the body. This becomes especially effective when applied by a practitioner who is attuned to the higher dimensions.

ADVANCED LIFE ENERGY

The term 'advanced life Energy', used throughout this book with a capital E, represents the unified field (subtle energies) transmitted through SOS processes that broadcast and register signals to every living thing and communicate within the mind and body on a cellular level.

Human beings have a basic energetic life force that is necessary for the support of life – 'advanced life Energy', as it is used in this book, *is not this energy*. What you will discover by applying the Stillness Session Technology is how these higher frequencies interact with your brain and body physiology to release blocks, expand, and maintain a natural heightened synergy of heart, mind and spirit. What this elegant field of potential offers is new information and solutions that evolve and benefit life:

After losing a high-paying job, a woman discovered unconscious childhood memories that had imprisoned her for years. Once these old issues were unlocked, it gave her courage, strength and a new sense of her own power. She then found an even better position where she was able to assist her clients to recognize their special skills and talents, as she had (see Simply, Powerfully, Beautiful in Part 5).

When discovering a depth of love he had never recognized within himself, and the self-worth that accompanied it, a film producer's career skyrocketed into higher accolades that had only been a distant dream. He was then set free to find the success that had eluded him for so long (see Elusive Dreams in Part 5).

SENSORY PROCESSES USED IN SOS

- **sound** (Stillness Sessions)
- **sight** (words, images)
- **touch** (physical transmission)
- **intention** (potency)

We can attune to the Energy of higher intelligence *through* the senses.[4] In ages past, ancient wisdom revealed that these invisible frequencies can be accessed in numerous ways. Ervin Laszlo, the brilliant author of 74 books translated into 20 languages, explains and theorizes in *Science and the Reenchantment of the Cosmos*: "Conscious experience is tantamount to looking at the world through five slits in the tower: the eye, the ear, the palate, the nose, and the surface of the skin. Yet this may not be the last word. Could it be possible to attain a broader view – to open the roof to the sky?"[5]

When we are given glimpses into a deeper dimension, the kind that doesn't seem to be constructed by our intellect, and is key to unlocking more knowledge than we have been able to perceive, we sometimes shut it down, because it is unfamiliar. Your engagement with this invisible Energy increases your capabilities.

The more this advanced life Energy is active within your mind and body, the stronger its capacity of regeneration and circulation. SOS Tools, Teachings and Technology convey subtle energies through:

SOUND
energetically
enhanced
Stillness Session
recordings

SIGHT
books
words
symbols

TOUCH
physical
transmission,
energy
meridians

INTENTION
magnifies
the field
of potential

POWER AS USED IN SOS

The meaning of *power* referenced in all SOS work is "… what uplifts, dignifies and ennobles."[6] It is not associated with *force* that creates counterforce, or resistance of any kind.

MATTER AND ENERGY

Matter is vibrating energy; human beings are a collection of vibrations – from our organs, to the brain, to all our cells – everything is vibrating. Anytime there is an energetic imbalance, there is disruption in the field, and a physical impairment or illness may manifest in some form or another. Any blockage in your body, whether from stress, trauma or emotional pain, halts the natural flow in the energy meridians of your physical body – and if not taken care of, future illnesses appear that are even more detrimental to your health and wellbeing. Therefore, having an ability to release the blockage in any of the areas that are not in tune, is like opening the gates of the dam. You develop harmony with frequencies of higher consciousness, like optimism, reverence and love. It gets you in the flow of life that naturally brings benefits to every day.

As this Energy of higher consciousness expands within, you get to participate in healing any past or recent emotional pain (*see Epigenetics, Part 3*). Healing these unconscious patterns impacts the course of your life. What is evidenced in these studies is not something we've been taught to believe is possible:

- *What could cause negative habits to shift that have been replayed in the subconscious mind for years?*

- *What could interact with the intelligent cellular structure in the body to create the various forms of healing evidenced?*

- *How can this level of healing occur across distances and when there is (often) no physical contact?*

One reason I included *Insights, Questions & Reflections* throughout this book is to slow down the lower mind's usual thought processes – and move into the higher mind's intuitive center by observing and reflecting on what is actually occurring that is out of the ordinary.

where the rubber meets the road

Bringing The SOS Method into the everyday of life is where the rubber meets the road. They are not practices that dissipate into the ethers the moment a baby cries or you lose your job. There is an extremely *practical* element to The Simplicity of Stillness; it involves walking this journey with the intention of connecting to your very soul, *while* transforming your greatest challenges. The more you integrate the Tools, Teachings and Technology into your life, the more rapidly you will see extraordinary benefits appearing.

Will your life suddenly be free of all troubles? Of course not, but you will know how to process them through a lens of clarity that brings better outcomes. As you discover how to focus on what is of greatest importance, your potential and purpose will appear through your energetic attunement. Myths once believed as 'truth' will be deconstructed, as will any concepts that inhibit evolutionary growth. Every day you'll notice challenges you might have considered daunting now being handled with ease.

What you learn *experientially* will redefine what is possible for you. There are many ways to begin, even a 21 day plan can bring about qualities synonymous with the vibration of higher consciousness impacting your thoughts and actions. Enthusiasm, inspiration, forgiveness, kindness and a general sense of wellbeing will be woven into your life as you step into this world.

CONNECT

While I was writing this part of the book, I found interesting interviews and research, and thanks to today's modern innovations I am able to share them with you. Just follow the link or scan the QR code and enjoy:

www.theSOSmethod.com/sosconnect1

 Watch a video of Mary Burmeister, Master of Jin Shin Jyutsu healing tradition

 Read articles on healing and purifying the body from ancient knowledge that influenced many present day wellness traditions worldwide

 Watch a video interview of Dr. William A. Tiller discussing his experiment on Intention

when you wake up knowing
there is wonder in life
there is

when you go to sleep believing
miracles can happen
they do

each day a mystery could unfold
that wasn't even considered before

find the knowing that places you
in this infinite river of life

let the rushing waters surround you
with what's truly possible
and it will be

only then can you see
the unconscious walls
that once imprisoned your heart

only then will you know
how to fly beyond them
and be free

when you wake up knowing
there is wonder in life
there is

Marlise Karlin

PART 2
THE SIMPLICITY OF
STILLNESS® METHOD
IN 3 SIMPLE STEPS

THE SIMPLICITY OF STILLNESS METHOD

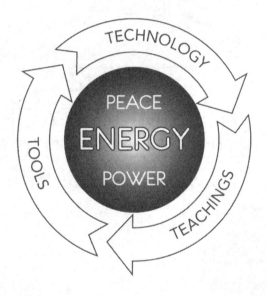

THE ELEMENTS

Stillness Sessions Technology – are the activating element

SOS Teachings – assist you in acquiring knowledge

SOS Tools – give you a directed focus

THE ELEMENTS

The Simplicity of Stillness is a modern, rapid and direct method of accessing the *sweet spot of life*, where deep peace and the flow of higher consciousness converge. The essential elements are:

Stillness Sessions Technology – transmits advanced life Energy (subtle energies) on waves of sound. These scientifically researched audio recordings of beautiful music and words activate deep peace and the flow of higher awareness.

SOS Teachings – a convergence of knowledge from ancient wisdom and Eastern healing traditions, with modern scientific research. This mind-expanding information supports you in acquiring beliefs that uplift and empower new life choices.

SOS Tools – assist you to directly focus in a specific area, instead of on the wide range of thoughts that normally fill the mind. This focus develops conscious habits that bring harmonious circumstances and events into daily life.

What is inherent within you is speaking louder than ever so you can recognize what is truly possible. As we all become more connected with this *"miracle that orchestrates every pulse of our existence,"*[1] it will shape the future in a way that is yet to be fully realized, igniting dreams once forgotten.

3 SIMPLE STEPS

1   APPLY

2   ACTIVATE

3   ACT

The Elements

1 APPLY SOS TOOL & TEACHING: Explore/review knowledge. Calm the mind. Directly focus on a specific area. Release self-defeating tendencies. Develop new life choices and habits. SOS Tools featured here are:
- **Release & Let Go**: eliminate blocks, generate new habits
- **Making Requests**: access knowledge and creative solutions
- **Expanding Intuitive Abilities**: accelerate capabilities beyond the mind
- **Transmitting Conscious Communication**: increase effectiveness through thinking, speaking and transmitting
- **Setting Potent Intentions**: generate creative though with potency

2 ACTIVATE ENERGY POTENTIAL THROUGH STILLNESS SESSIONS TECHNOLOGY: Accelerate healing, creativity and higher awareness in your mind, body and spirit. Learn from the inside out. Experiential wisdom accelerates through transmission of advanced life Energy. Stillness Session formats include:
- **Deep State Stillness Session** (meditative)
- **Elevate Session** (vitality)
- **Sacred Word Session** (invocation)
- **DNA Healing Session**

3 ACT ON INSPIRATION AS IT IS REVEAED: Extraordinary abilities, talents and qualities appear when you take action from inspiration. Follow through to develop the life you envision. Your intention and commitment guides the momentum. By practicing daily, you will find more love, beauty and empowerment appearing, which brings greater hope, healing and happiness into your life.

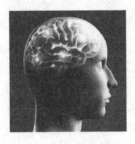

BRAIN

imprints new
neural pathways

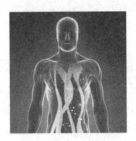

BODY

releases blocked
cellular memory

SPIRIT

activates advanced
Energy of higher
consciousness

WHAT, WHERE & WHY

WHAT SOS DOES

The Simplicity of Stillness is a comprehensive method that activates advanced levels of healing Energy into your life. It has the potential to heal depression, post-traumatic stress disorder (PTSD), addictions, fibromyalgia and chronic illnesses in the following ways:

- **BRAIN**: Imprints new neural pathways

- **BODY**: Releases blocked cellular memory in the body

- **SPIRIT**: Activates Energy of higher consciousness

What is experienced in the moment is not indicative of the (causal and etheric) healing taking place. How you evidence it is through better health, more heart-felt relationships, a career you enjoy and greater prosperity.

WHERE IT COMES FROM

The Simplicity of Stillness is synthesized from 20 years of study and research in Eastern wisdom and healing traditions, The New Science, and experiential learning. Integrating research from a decade of case studies that evidenced mental, emotional, physical, and spiritual benefits has inspired new technologies to continually be developed.

WHY IT IS SO BENEFICIAL

A deeper and immediate sense of inner peace is reported by 96.5 percent of people. Applying SOS daily offers numerous benefits, where you:

- Begin living in the flow of life

- Know how to find possibility in the midst of adversity

- Enjoy the remarkable synchronistic events that appear

- Define a life of greater flexibility, ease and joy from the new conscious habits you have developed

SIMPLE, RAPID, DIRECT

My intention in developing SOS was to make the tools and technology so enjoyable that you include it as a daily practice in your life. It takes a certain level of curiosity and inspiration to try something new. And if, like most people, you lead a busy life, then you are also looking for something that is simple, accessible, powerful and enjoyable.

Many people practice Stillness Sessions daily as they are the elemental icing on the cake that gives you concrete evidence of how quickly you can find peace, become more confident, and discover skills you never realized you have. Using audio recordings makes it easy to incorporate into each day, and the Energy field it transmits assures that it will always contain remarkable levels of effectiveness.

What you aim for becomes possible, whether it's cultivating new ideas, releasing remnants of emotional pain, accessing intuitive abilities, or having more love in your life. Who wouldn't want that? I do. I guess that's why I continually practice it myself. What this gift offers us all is a level of transformation it's time to recognize and cultivate … more and more each day.

a man

born blind can easily

deny the magnificence of a vast landscape

he can easily deny all the wonders that he cannot

touch, smell, taste, or hear

but one day the wind will show you its kindness

and remove the patches that

cover your eyes

Meister Eckhart
German theologian, philosopher and mystic

PART 3
THE NEW SCIENCE

EPIGENETICS, THE PETRI DISH OF LIFE
genetic environments – past, present & future

According to conventional science, our genetic inheritance is set in stone – it is our DNA that solely determines our health, personality traits and intelligence. Like a roll of the dice, you get what you came in with, and that's it. Many people still believe this today. But discoveries have been made that confound previous research; a simple change in environment can turn your genes on or off. What this suggests is that your genes, like a computer, await instructions from your *software* to tell them what to do. As scientists delve into the Software of Life,[1] they are consistently revealing new, mindboggling features of the cellular world.

The word 'epi' comes from the Greek language meaning over, above, outer, therefore epigenetics means 'on top of' genetics. Epigenetics is the study of changes in gene expression caused by mechanisms other than changes in the underlying DNA sequence. Another way to look at it is that DNA is a language (which it is), and the epigenome formats that language. The epigenome can remember how it formats text and can replicate it again and again.

Stem biologist Dr. Bruce Lipton gained a different perspective when he saw what happened to a genetically identical cell that had been split into three Petri dishes. He placed each one in a different culture medium, the (environment) chemistry in which cells grow. In one they formed muscle, in another bone, and in the third dish they formed fat cells. "This was so mindboggling because here I am, teaching in the classroom that genes control life, and in the laboratory, the cells are revealing to me that genes don't control it at all! It's the *environment* that controls the fate of the cells."[2] It was a determining moment that shifted Dr. Lipton's entire life.

determining factors of your cell inheritance

Scientists discovered that a switch can be turned on in a gene by the environment – and *the memory* (cellular) and its physiological effect can be passed forward to future generations. This is a radical departure from the fundamental belief that your environment *(emotional experiences, thoughts, beliefs and physical environment)* is never passed on – only the genes. It was something many scientists considered impossible because it would mean that what you *experience* would not only affect you but your children, and possibly future generations as well.

Considering this, you begin to realize that the state of mind; the thoughts, words and emotional as well as physical environment of your ancestry could have a psychological and behavioral effect on your entire life. Your predisposition toward anxiety and/or adventure, your weaknesses *and/or* strengths, could have been influenced by your grandparents' and parents' environment. These tendencies, once noted, can become part of your journey to heal, *and* to access your greatest qualities. What you will discover through the

New Science is an extraordinary potential – instead of a life sentence, a framework of evidence that suggests we are not powerless, and can define a new future for our lives as well as our children's.

feast or famine and its effects

Marcus Pembrey, clinical geneticist at the Institute of Child Health at University College, London, and Lars Olov Bygren LD, Umea University, Sweden, carried out research that provided information on how environmental events could affect our genes and be passed to future generations.[3] They found that cycles of famine and harvest influenced the health of the offspring of people living in an isolated village in Sweden 100 years later, even though *they never experienced the famine themselves*.

One impact the study demonstrated showed a significant coherency between generations – between the diet in one and the health of their children and grandchildren in another. Their findings complemented other studies on epigenetics and revealed that it is possible for something other than DNA to move between the generations.

inherited stress

Jonathan Seckl, a geneticist at the University of Edinburgh, was working on a research project into how the stress on a mother during pregnancy could affect her children. The initial research was with rats.[4] What it showed him was completely unexpected. The offspring of a highly anxious pregnant mother had altered stress responses *for the rest of their lifespan.* These effects continued to be carried by babies born several generations in the future! What he discovered evidenced that the genes were *switched on* in successive generations, each having similar levels of the chemical properties inherent in those with high states of anxiety.

Rachel Yehuda, a psychiatrist at the Mt. Sinai School of Medicine, was also convinced of transgenerational stress from a study of the children of holocaust survivors. Even during adulthood, they demonstrated having the effects of the stress, apparently, from the continual retelling of their parents' traumatic stories while growing up. She decided to team up with Seckl and study pregnant women who were directly and emotionally affected by the tragedy of September 11 2001 in New York City.[5]

When people are exposed to a stressful event they produce cortisol, a hormone that helps *counteract* the response to stress (i.e. cortisol helps to lower adrenaline surges caused by stress). What Yehuda and Seckl found is that 50 percent of the women who developed post-traumatic stress disorder (PTSD) after 9/11 had low levels of cortisol in their saliva i.e. their body didn't produce enough to help them emotionally deal with the situation. The most striking discovery in their research was that the babies of these women also had low levels of cortisol

What the results of these studies, and many more, brought into view is how the biochemical effect *of a traumatic event can travel through generations.* Regardless of what you know of your lineage, there has been violence and war, pain and suffering in the world for eons. We all carry different levels of stress and the cellular memory of suffering experienced by our ancestry. We also carry the nurturing, resilient, and adventurous mental and emotional *environments* of our lineage, but they don't present the challenges that leave molecular scars – those that can also be attributed to alcoholic or abusive parents. How can this be healed? What can resolve these issues?

the alchemy of healing

Your cells are incredibly intelligent – they can heal a cut or produce the chemicals needed to calm anxiety, but can they independently heal the memory embedded from generational or recent pain? From all I have studied – through the healing arts, ancient teachings, science and SOS case histories, this only happens through the alchemy of infinite conscious Energy as it circulates through the cellular structures in your body. This is why people who achieved advanced meditative states were able to release past suffering and not live with the mental and physical effects it can cause.

Marcus Pembrey, who worked for many years in the field of clinical and molecular genetics, felt deeply moved after making discoveries about epigenetics. He believes we are each the guardian of our genome – that we are meant to take care of it in this life by taking care of ourselves, and by choosing the environment we want to be surrounded by.

Not everyone agrees with these scientific findings, even though today considerably more studies have been done, but imagine what we could miss out on that could be of great value, by not looking deeper. It's important to become aware of belief systems that might have been handed down by cultural or societal beliefs in any area of life they might exist. As mentioned earlier, Dr. Ignaz Semmelweis developed an important discovery, the antiseptic procedures used today that have saved so many lives, and yet he was scorned throughout his entire life.[6] It's not easy to pioneer new thinking, but there are many today, like you, who have braved the tide and ventured into these exciting and turbulent waters.

Imagine the difference it could make if you could live without the impact these silent thieves have in your life. Your DNA does not have to determine your life; you can use this knowledge and the access you have to infinitely intelligent Energy to break the binds that hold you. What I have been convinced of from my research is how subtle energies can release cellular memories to bring about a high level of coherence in the mind and body.

This advanced life force found in the SOS processes heals the past through the alchemy of its presence. People experience a sense of freedom that vastly alters their mental, physical and emotional wellbeing. It clears away the debris of lifetimes. The case studies you read in this book demonstrate how this can happen, how you can release unconscious cellular memory, and open pathways to continually heal and move into higher levels of consciousness. The 3 Step process details how simply you can access this in your life as well.

The thoughts you think, the words you speak, and the actions you take, are the 'environment', the Petri dish of your life that will be carried forward to future generations. Understanding this and the phenomenal possibilities to heal and become fully empowered can make a tremendous difference in your life today.

DNA, YOUR GENES DON'T DEFINE YOU
the wonder of frequency and sound

The mind-body connection has always been a great fascination to me, fostered by personal health challenges at various times throughout my life. As a child, I had asthma and yearly bronchial illnesses that were so bad I had to be kept out of school for a month at a time. When I left home at 16, I never had another bout, not even a wheeze. In later years, twice when I spoke about my father, I was so angry that my body reacted violently – the first time it happened in six hours, the next time in only one. I curled into a fetal position from the horrific pain I was in as I waited for the ambulance and the morphine to lower the intensity of my suffering. It would calm me in the moment, but it didn't take it away – the anger, the illness or the agony.

Why was this happening? Was there a relationship between what I thought, what I said, and my body's reaction? Were there other factors involved?

My earliest studies to find answers were through master teachers of ancient wisdom, meditation, and various healing traditions. What I discovered soothed my mind and began to heal my body – and while it wasn't like anything I had learned from conventional education or the traditional model of medicine I grew up with, it made sense to me. And it worked. My health got better, my life got happier, and I learned to stay open to new ideas.

The journey continued and my curiosity to understand even more grew into a hunger. New science from those daring to challenge conventional models began to appear in the books I read, which often matched or explained the ancient teachings I had absorbed, but in an entirely different way. Then experts in various scientific fields began appearing in my life. The universe seemed to be deliberately conspiring to bring me in close contact with knowledge that would later inspire The Simplicity of Stillness Method. It resulted in a marriage of sorts; unifying the study of scientific research with the experiential knowledge I gained from the depths of my inward journey, all provoking even deeper questioning.

What I encountered through the years and then in the SOS Scientific Study (*see Appendix*) intensified my inquisitive nature. Many of the outcomes defied conventional knowledge. I wanted to find the science that could assist people to understand what was happening to them, not only through the remarkable events they personally experienced, but to possibly explain how limiting patterns might have caused their pain. Were they all a result of recent or childhood circumstances? Or was something else at play? Oh, the mind loves to have answers, doesn't it?

rivers of knowledge converge in oceans of exploration

My research led me deeper, and what I began to see is how the recent scientific findings of *Epigenetics, Neuroplasticity DNA, and Subtle Energies are intricately woven together, sparking an ever expansive frontier*. This is why I decided to focus specifically on these areas, as the science in each will facilitate remarkable discoveries in the future – for medicine and the practice of the healing arts. I believe it will assist us in recognizing the inherent power we've always had.

An article on generational pain (that exists in the cellular structure of the body), in *Discover Magazine* written by Dan Hurley,[1] an award-winning science journalist, reflects the wisdom of ancient wisdom and healing texts. Hurley wrote his findings when studying behavioral epigenetics, a new field that has become so stimulating it's contributing to numerous medical studies of treatments for healing the brain:

"According to the new insights of behavioral epigenetics, traumatic experiences in our past, or in our recent ancestors' past, leave molecular scars adhering to our DNA. Jews whose great-grandparents were chased from their Russian shtetls; Chinese whose grandparents lived through the ravages of the Cultural Revolution; young immigrants from Africa whose parents survived massacres; adults of every ethnicity who grew up with alcoholic or abusive parents — all carry with them more than just memories. Like silt deposited on the cogs of a finely tuned machine after the seawater of a tsunami recedes, our experiences, and those of our forebears, are never gone, even if they have been forgotten. They become a part of us, a molecular residue holding fast to our genetic scaffolding."

tendencies & possibilities

While psychological and behavioral tendencies can be inherited, they do not have to rule your life. When you advance your connection with the life-giving Energy inherent in each of us, it demonstrates there are no 'boxes' we have to live in. Your potential is limitless; I hope this chapter will clarify this for you.

When you reflect on any tendencies you have that don't seem to make sense – getting answers will feel like a piece of the puzzle has fallen into place. It can help you to understand yourself more (*see From Anger & Expectation to Acceptance & Forgiveness, Part 4*). Could these tendencies have been transferred down from a parent or grandparent? This knowledge can free you to be kind to yourself and to others who might be locked in patterns they can't yet see. Whatever limitations you feel you have, this healing process can bring tremendous relief. Remember, *you are the guardian of your future, and that of your lineage*. What do you want to pass on? Your influence can make a difference in the lives of those you love today, as well as in the future.

The energy field that you are is compliant, and as we become more conscious and coherent, the benefits become apparent throughout your life. The ancient healing arts have long recognized the body's innate capability to heal, ancient wisdom has written of the coherency of what activates it, and now science has discovered what verifies it – that our genetic codes are not a life sentence! Your DNA can change! When the Russian biophysicist and molecular biologist Pjotr Garjajev and his colleagues explored the vibrational behavior of DNA, they proved that DNA can be reprogrammed through words and frequencies.[2]

DNA is a digital code. It has four letters instead of two in binary computer code. The information encoded into DNA staggers the imagination. From the point of view of what is encapsulated within each cell of your body, in the DNA, is enough information in a half teaspoon to store all of the assembly instructions for every creature ever made, and room left over to include every book ever written! The information content of a bacterium (microscopic life form) has been estimated to be around 10,000,000,000,000 bits of information comparable to a hundred million pages of *Encyclopedia Britannica*.[3] This is the language of life that is encoded within each one of us.

DNA programming

An experiment performed by Garjajev's team that was as astonishing as significant, clarified they could reprogram DNA in living organisms by using the correct resonant frequencies of DNA. Which means, our DNA can be reprogrammed by *frequencies of human speech and sound, supposing that the words and sounds are modulated on the correct carrier frequencies.*

While I don't want to give away the story and the unexpected discoveries that were realized in *Defining New Horizons (see Part 4)*, what it clarified was the high level of impact that can happen when Energies not defined by our present physical domain, are coupled on the sound wave frequencies of words and music. It later inspired the development of specialized processes – uniquely different Stillness Session formats – that were given to people in the scientific study to include in the every day of their lives. What it demonstrated was extraordinary. We'll review this together in later chapters.

In summarizing the Russian's findings, authors Grazyna Fosar and Franz Bludors stated, "Of course the frequency has to be correct. And this is why everybody is not equally successful or can do it with always the same strength. The individual person must work on the inner processes in order to establish a conscious communication with the DNA."[4] This statement aligns with the research on subtle energies – that it is this force, which can be *carried* on the frequencies of sound and words, that produces change in DNA. What's important to realize, is that connecting to this healing power is within your reach. Renowned bestselling author Dr. Wayne Dyer, *There's a Spiritual Solution to Every Problem*[5], and Dr. Valery V. Hunt, *Infinite Mind: Science of the Human Vibrations of Consciousness*[6] indicate similar thoughts about the importance of attuning with inner processes to accelerate your vibrational frequency:

- "As you begin to consider this idea of faster vibrations being synonymous with spirit, remind yourself that we live in a world of invisible energy." – Wayne Dyer (unified field)

- "When a person's field reached higher vibrational states, he experienced knowing higher information, transcendental ideas, insight about ultimate sources of reality, and creativity in its purest form." – Valery Hunt (the more you connect with higher energetic information, your innate intelligence accelerates)

When Dr. David Hawkins was asked "If Truth is formless, how can it be conveyed through words?", his response was, "It is the formless that accompanies the form of words which accounts for the transmission" and "The energy field of the teacher is a manifestation of the Presence. It is that field that accounts for the miraculous ..."[7] What DNA research is making available is that our genes do not define us. The evidence of generational predisposition to illness, personality and physical traits can be redefined in ways that set markers of possibility instead of constraints. We are not living in a world defined by the limitations we once considered to be facts.

I personally believe that by combining the best of all worlds; harmonizing with the intelligent Energy field, including the latest scientific discoveries in modern medicine, and the application of ancient healing arts – will exponentially increase wellbeing. Many more people are moving toward this understanding, some traditional doctors as well. The tide is slowly but surely turning. The development and maintenance of this advanced life force Energy is one of the best sources of health today.

What I hope and intend for you to discover is the power you have to tap into that deep knowing within and find what works best for you. As you connect to higher levels of consciousness, all the answers are there, all the guidance you will ever need. I have witnessed extraordinary events people drew into their lives as they became empowered by this cohesive knowledge.

What this reveals and can open for you is a future of uncompromising potential, one that you can begin living in now. So many of the discoveries that science is bringing to light today just confirm the wondrous and impressive abilities inherent in each of us. The information in the next chapters will clarify this even more. The journey continues!

BRAIN POWER
the elegant genius of neuroplasticity

Absolutely incredible! Extraordinary discoveries in science are knocking down more walls of entrenched views that have made us feel victim to the ravages of time and our heritage. Another limiting belief filtered down through the centuries has been eliminated. We are *not* stuck with the brain we were born with, and it does not have to diminish as we get older.

Neuroplasticity is a word you want to get to know; it describes newly discovered breakthroughs that *your brain can change*!! WOW!! Think of the fears that arise when you think you have no choice; that what you've been told for years, as defeating as it might be – is *just the way it is*. Similar to your genetic makeup, science has now proven what ancient wisdom and the healing arts have always known: that you have the power to change – your brain as well as what has been passed down to you genetically. Your brain and your genetic makeup can be altered!

The predominant theory was that an adult brain is immutable i.e. it cannot change – that we did not have the capability to replace the daily loss of brain cells with new ones. A milestone happened in neuroscience in 1998 when a study revealed that the brain has the ability to develop new brain cells and that nerves can continually rearrange themselves throughout the course of life.[1] The physiology of the brain changes in direct response to experiential learning. New connections can form at any stage!

What this means is that we can develop new ways of thinking and behaving! Past events in your personal life that have caused you to become defensive, internalize hurts and behave in ways that don't match who you believe yourself to be – don't have to hold you hostage anymore. Those emotions become repetitious patterns that set grooves in the brain, where it's easy to become angry and inflict pain or retribution. We all know the warning signs, they appear seemingly out of nowhere, and soon you're reacting to situations in ways that don't align with your true values.

It's possible for those patterns to be replaced through the brain's plasticity, your repetitious thoughts and actions. Synaptic pruning enables neural connections that are *not used* on a regular basis to be removed so more useful connections can be strengthened. This happens through connection to the Energy field that releases those patterns and sets new ways of thinking, habits and behavior in place (*see case studies and stories*). Negative patterns of consistent anxiety, anger, obsession or jealousy passed down from generational memory or childhood events, which might have supported the development of those neural pathways, can actually die off.

What does this mean for you? We all know how incredibly difficult it is to change behavior. Even when you are committed, there are triggers that set off emotional and chemical responses. What makes it possible to dissolve, or lessen, these automatic reactive impulses so they can be removed, or *pruned*, granting the greater you to be revealed? Two women scientists who are specialists, one in the field of brain biochemistry, the other a neuroanatomist, had this to say:

Dr. Candace Pert, the late former Chief of the Section on Brain Biochemistry of the Clinical Neuroscience Branch of the National Institute of Mental Health (NIMH), spoke about her personal discoveries:

"It's ironic because I'm a neuroscientist, and I studied the brain because I thought by studying the brain I would understand how to feel good, how to lead a happy life, unlock the mysteries of the universe. But now what I'm really interested in is in consciousness. And what my research at the NIMH revealed, is that yes *the brain is important but consciousness is beyond the brain.*"[2]

This ties in with the revelatory information Dr. Jill Bolte Taylor, a Harvard-trained neuroanatomist, received while having a massive stroke in the left hemisphere of her brain. In her book, *My Stroke of Insight*, Jill reported her experience to be of a physical nature that pierced the paralyzed state she was in, alternating between euphoria and a sense of complete wellbeing and peace.[3] It was an extremely perilous situation but it gave her access to an experience beyond the constraints of everyday reality. This experience was so powerful it reconstructed her way of thinking and became a turning point in her life.

What both of these scientists discovered is the importance of connecting with conscious awareness beyond the mind. The Energy field of infinite intelligence is essential to shift those pesky patterns from the past, and set new neural pathways in the brain, so you can "feel good, lead a happy life, and unlock the mysteries of the universe." The vast capabilities of the mind become clearer as we bring all the necessary elements together.

During Jill's recovery, the neuroplasticity of her brain supported her to regain the many abilities she had lost during her stroke. She had to learn even the basics of tying her shoes and getting dressed. Eventually she reclaimed the brilliance of her mind to reconstruct all that happened, write a book about it, and teach others about neuroplasticity and the deepest knowing within that guided her back.

And so we find again the purpose for incorporating these powerful elements, The New Science of Neuroplasticity, Epigenetics and DNA, with advanced life Energy. The more adept we become at activating knowledge beyond the constraints of mind, to advance our mind's capabilities – by connecting with this unifying flow – the more we can move into ways of living that benefit our personal lives and society as a whole.

the effects of your environment

Brain research was conducted in the early 1950s to understand whether environment had any effect on the structure and function of the brain. Adult animals were divided into two groups; one exposed to an enriched environment, and one decidedly less. The enriched environments led to new brain cell development in the hippocampus (the structure critical to new learning and memory) of the animals. It confirmed the effects of plasticity in the cerebral cortex.[4] It's interesting, isn't it, how 'environment' and neuroplasticity work in conjunction with each other, demonstrating again the relevance of reviewing these sciences simultaneously.

Dr. Robert Sapolsky, a Stanford University neurobiologist, was working on a scientific study with baboons years later, when a seemingly catastrophic incident proved to be fortuitous. It increased the understanding of the level of change possible regarding the effect of the environment on brain structure. An entire community accidentally ate tainted food, killing off many in the troop, including the alpha males. Those remaining were much gentler, and more compassionate. As new members joined the community in the coming years, they would adapt to the existing behavior in the troop. Even if they were alpha, within six months they would also become kinder like the rest of the baboons.[5]

What their uniquely different behavior suggests is that it's possible to change well-established patterns. Did the new behavior the baboons demonstrated happen because of more cellular connections (synapsis) and the formation of new brain cells (neurogenesis) in the hippocampus, similar to findings in the 1950s' study? Could this also indicate that new neural pathways were paved in the brains of the baboons new to the community that led to this phenomenal change?

What Sapolsky's study ultimately demonstrated is that it's possible to transform an entire social system in less than a generation. By eliminating high levels of stress, it's possible to have a society that not only survives, but thrives on peaceful and more compassionate behavior. This study's focus was to advance understanding of stress, but what it also demonstrated is how, when longstanding patterns like domination and aggression are eliminated, it results in a profound behavioral shift (throughout the existing society). The possibilities this represents are those worth contemplating. As we each become more conscious and caring, will this effect get passed on to those around us?

expanding or diminishing compassion

The well-known study of 10 Buddhist monks and 10 volunteers asked to meditate on compassion for a week, revealed an increase in gamma wave (a pattern of neural oscillation) production in the brains of all the monks, and only two of the volunteers.[6]

The monks had previously meditated on compassion for more than 10,000 hours and the volunteers had just learned to meditate. *This is why consistent practice is advised to form those pathways that stimulate your brain to remember and make it simpler to return to new behavior.* And, the average wave production didn't decrease in the monks once meditation stopped. Which makes it appear that you can *retain* higher vibrational qualities, i.e. the Energy frequencies you connect with do not dissipate.

As we evolve into higher levels of consciousness, patterns of pride, anger, blame and indifference are replaced by new qualities. As your energetic frequency moves higher, you embrace optimism, acceptance, willingness and love, and the new pathways set in the brain support your continual return to these qualities and unifying habits. The unconscious patterns that imprisoned you at one time, cycling round in repetitious grooves, do not have to determine your life destiny. This is where neuroplasticity really makes its mark!

Scientists continue to probe the limits of neuroplasticity and what they are finding is breaking down layers of concepts we took to be facts. Misdirected information given as fact has led to many decisions and treatments, or none, that affect people's lives with trauma and mental health challenges. What has seemed hopeless, regarding addiction, depression, emotional trauma, brain injury, and various illnesses, now, through these discoveries, can change (*see The Relentless Pain of Being a Hero, Part 7*, and stories in *The Power of Peace In You*).[7] There is a glimmer on the horizon and it is getting brighter each day.

ingenious, inspired health in the 21st century

I am not suggesting that simply learning about the various discoveries throughout this chapter can cure illness. There is a marked difference between a *cure* and a *healing* (*see Ancient Art & The New Science*). But the belief *you* have of what is possible makes an enormous difference in the knowledge, practices and circumstances you draw into your life.

Insight infused by infinite guidance will always inspire the best care possible – and that could be a melding of modern medicine with various healing therapies. In the SOS Scientific Study *(see Appendix)*, some people had found doctors who listened to them, who were open to hearing their patient's ideas, and would support the integration of various forms of healthcare. And there were cases of people who had stopped going to their doctors, because they felt so depressed by them – their attitude, uncaring nature, and one-pointed focus on having the only opinion that mattered.

It doesn't have to be like this. There are more doctors today that are open to walking a journey of wellbeing with you; who will give you their expertise and work alongside you to incorporate your ideas and suggestions. How The Simplicity of Stillness assists you is by offering tools and technology that powerfully connect you with that vital life stream that continually inspires the best decisions. Your inner knowing can offer you insight beyond what you imagine, which includes listening to expert advice from various schools of thought, going within, hearing the messages given, and taking action.

Allow the profound to guide you to the practical. Without bringing this intelligence into everyday, making the daily decisions required by life can be quite difficult.

messages and persistence

On the day I began writing this chapter, a bird flew directly into one of the glass doors in my living room where I was writing. He began tapping with his beak, as though he wanted to enter. The bird didn't stop, but went from door to door, flapping his wings. My feathered messenger returned on the second day, repeating the pattern. And returned again on the third, fourth, fifth and sixth day. I took it as a sign to become still, to look and see if more information would be uncovered that was essential to this chapter.

Was there more that I hadn't fully grasped? The answer wasn't immediately forthcoming. I reflected on what I wanted to clarify – how beliefs can block us from our true potential – how the mind is willing and ready to assist us at every turn. And, the message that came through is that it is up to each of us to persist, to access the experiential wisdom that breaks down the barriers, to apply the knowledge gained, and invite the brilliance of our mind to assist us in this evolutionary journey.

The brain can change as a result of the thoughts we think. A simple thought can alter neural connections. An enlivened mind is so elegantly genius it's hard to comprehend. And, the reality is, if we don't shift thought patterns from the lower tendencies, nothing will change. The cost in lost creativity, productivity and the disintegration of love in our relationships is staggering.

Can we be as persistent as that little bird? Will you find the discipline to return again and again to what delivers a world where there are solutions to whatever challenges you, where there is more love than drops in the ocean, more peace than grains of sand in the desert? Only you can answer this question.

breathe, listen and shift

You might have noticed the blue pages placed throughout the book; they are inset as reminders to go within. Anytime you feel that dropping down sensation that occurs when Stillness wants to take you home – let it. The universal awareness that implicitly inspires and invokes the wisdom of the ages is always just a breath away. The neural pathways that have inset negative programming are diminished each time you breathe deep and connect with this Energy field of infinite brilliance.

My suggestion is to go to the Just For You Stillness Session Page (*see Part 4*), download or send for the various Stillness Session recordings that can activate this connection now. Keep them handy – place them in your cell phone as well as your computer – and use them as frequently as you like. Even now, your ability to advance your brain power is calling you to listen from the Stillness within.

CONNECT

This is one of the most exciting areas of the 'New Science'. What I have written about is what I find to be the most important aspects of Epigenetics, DNA and Neuroplasticity – and I thought you would enjoy hearing from the experts or reading a bit more. Follow the link or scan the QR code to dive into their extensive knowledge:

www.theSOSmethod.com/sosconnect2

 Listen to the recording of a Bruce Lipton Interview with Marlise that gives you great analogies on Epigenetics and so much more

 Watch a video of a William A. Tiller Interview with Marlise discussing what is beyond distance time, this expansive Energy field, and that deep knowing

 Read articles from leading authorities in their fields like Carl Sagan, Dr. Gabor Mate, and Jill Bolte Taylor Ph.D.

A mind

once expanded by
a new idea

never returns

to its original
dimensions

Oliver Wendell Holmes Sr,
American physician, poet, professor and author

PART 4
STILLNESS SESSIONS® TECHNOLOGY

SOUND, SUBTLE ENERGIES & STILLNESS SESSIONS
igniting coherence

The capabilities of what subtle energies offer for healing, igniting higher consciousness, and creating coherence in the mind and body, have yet to gain wide understanding or recognition. It is a frontier waiting to be discovered that will advance humanity's capabilities to new levels. Inherent in all, this capacity for evolving consciousness and the body's self-healing abilities is a future worth attaining.

David Hawkins, M.D. Ph.D. renowned physician, researcher and author writes about his own experiences in *Power vs. Force* and the phenomenal benefits attuning to this awareness brought into his and other people's lives.[1] The effects were tangible. Others have also recorded how these invisible energy patterns can travel tremendous distances as these energies are not locked into distance-time as we know it. The energy patterns have also been used on devices specifically invented to develop physical evidence[2] and the effects have been remarkable. This area has yet to be fully utilized and will, I imagine, one day bring untold benefits.

How subtle energies move through the senses was discussed in *Energy & Awareness (see Part 1)*, now let's look deeper into sound.

SOUND

Sound and electromagnetic waves are used in many applications of daily life:

- **Sound waves** are formed by the disturbance of air particles.

- **Electromagnetic waves** are formed through electric and magnetic fields (radio, cell tower, TV).

- **Every wave** has a specific wavelength *(although there are no devices at this time that can measure subtle energies)*.

- **Sound waves vary in wavelength** according to the pitch of the sound.

- **Electromagnetic waves** vary greatly in wavelength, from radio waves, to visible light, and X-rays.[3]

- **Frequency** is used to measure the wavelength over time.

- **All waves** transfer energy.

sound resonance

Sound resonance is an invisible interaction between waves, particles and your senses, where the higher, more powerful order of energy harmonizes a new rhythm. Simple examples most people are familiar with are tuning forks. Physical resonance occurs when two objects have frequencies of oscillations that are close to each other. When two such systems are in proximity, they will resonate at the frequency dictated by the stronger of the two.[4]

sound healing and therapy

Sound has become an accepted form of therapy. It is well known that appropriate resonant music can calm the mind and decrease anxiety; it is used for dementia and autism, in surgery centers, airplanes, and in varied locations to produce these results.

'Sound healing' uses diverse frequencies delivered through tuning forks, crystal bowls, music and myriad devices to bring the mind and body into resonant vibrations of greater health and harmony. Some of the devices that produce sound waves measure stress and relaxation parameters to *play back* the signals to guide and *steer* the user into a relaxed state. This applied science is used to entrain brave wave states of Beta, Alpha, Theta and Delta that are known to evoke feelings of calm and serenity. All of these applications offer varying benefits.

HOW SUBTLE ENERGIES USE SOUND

To understand the new frontier being discovered today, let's talk about the difference between wavelengths. 'Subtle energies' are invisible like sound and electromagnetic waves – and, they can be carried on a sound wave – yet they are uniquely different. *Sound and electromagnetic waves are measurable. Subtle energies are not.*

According to Dr. Tiller, machines have yet to be developed that can measure the distances these forces can extend. The Vedic wisdom tradition, Eastern healing, and now the New Science are all calling out for us to reconnect to this unseen knowledge and the power it offers.

Stillness Sessions are a next-generation technology that transmit advanced life Energy (subtle energies) on carrier waves of sound. I developed these scientifically researched audio recordings of music and words to connect you to the creative power in you whether you are at work, on the move, or at home. What is so extraordinary is that

YOUR MIND DOES NOT HAVE TO BECOME STILL FOR IT TO WORK.

Whether you've struggled to meditate or are a lifelong meditator, this technology impacts your life by rapidly connecting you to the potential that heals your mind and body, while releasing anxiety and stress. Stillness Sessions can be integrated easily into your existing practice, or can become your core connection practice.

Originally they were developed to access advanced meditative states. Over the last year, the technology evolved to include the various formats that *activate your potential without having to be in meditation*. When given to people in the Scientific Study (*see Appendix 1*) as well as on the last Simplicity of Stillness tour, it became evident that these new recordings demonstrated similar effects without deep meditation. When using these formats, you can:

1. Keep your eyes open or closed.
2. Listen at work, on a walk, or while driving.
3. Elevate your state to the next level, from neutral to vitality and inspiration, or from depression to hopefulness.

Transcending conventional beliefs, people had exceptional insights and received healing benefits in sometimes as little as four and seven minutes. The *new* Stillness Sessions formats include:

- **Elevate Session:** Elevates baseline emotional state with vitality. An inspirational pick-me-up for finding new solutions.

- **Sacred Word Session:** Invocation developed using the underlying DNA language of word frequency for self-repetition.

- **DNA Healing Session:** Circulates harmonious energies for sound and word healing. Uplifting musical content for playing in the *background* of your life, at work or at play.

And the original:

- **Deep State Stillness:** Activates meditative states that develop coherence of mind-body-spirit. Accesses rare experiences of Stillness, invokes illumined understanding.

Included with this book are three Stillness Sessions of different lengths; Deep State Stillness, Elevate and a Sacred Word Session. They are instantly downloadable by following the instructions on the *Just For You – Stillness Sessions* page at the end of this section. If you prefer to receive a CD, you can find out how to do that there as well.

Stillness Sessions Technology impacts your life from the first time you listen. The benefits spoken of in this book occur by applying this technology and the tools that bring new habits into your life. The Simplicity of Stillness is a cohesive method, each element adds to the whole. It brings a higher energetic connection into the practical of everyday reality – your work, social and family life. Consciously maintaining this experience throughout the day continually expands consciousness within, not only to benefit you, but what you soon discover is that your influence reaches a much broader spectrum as well.

DEFINING NEW HORIZONS
from Tahiti's sun-kissed shores

Energy. What does it mean to you? For years most people defined it as vitality, heart-pounding strength, a winning personality or charisma. Today, it is generally acknowledged that the entire universe consists of energy and so do we. While this is a fact, it can be difficult for the mind to imagine. What it defines is that our world is composed of elements beyond what the naked eye can see, the ear can hear, and intellectual knowledge can grasp.

There are scientists and philosophers throughout time who have realized the vast capabilities of this invisible world, and researched various ways to evidence the discoveries they would one day make known. Unbeknownst to me, I would soon discover revelations of a similar nature, although researched in a laboratory less conventional than most. I was on my way to Tahiti.

An engineer, who had an exceptional experience in an SOS program, had asked if he might assist in producing my first Stillness Session recording. He completed it just in time, delivering the CD as I took off for the airport. I'm sure he never imagined all that would happen from his kind gesture. Events that would unravel the depth, power and mystery the higher Energies consciousness has to offer, converged on a day that appeared like any another. What was demonstrated clarified much of what we are meant to understand of this invisible world when the time is ripe.

night to day, black to white

I was inspired to listen to the newly made recording, one cloudy morning, and extended an invitation to my host. It was set to become an interesting gathering, if only from the participants who had given their consent to attend. My host, Tamahere, had conveyed upon my arrival that he didn't believe whatsoever in what I was teaching or what this 'stillness' was about. He asked if two young missionaries, who he said had been at his home 'proselytizing', could join him. Rounding out the group was a National Geographic photographer, who was traveling with me to document the many faces of stillness.

I put the CD on the dilapidated player Tamahere provided, and within no time I was in agony. Something was terribly wrong. The recording sounded really bad; the music was scratchy and my words weren't clear. In the short time I had been doing this work, I had learned to go with the flow, allow things to unfold, and so I did, for another few minutes – until I couldn't take it any longer. I decided I would ask my host if he had another player, maybe that would fix the problem.

When I looked in their direction, I couldn't believe what I saw. Everyone's eyes were closed; their faces revealed what they were experiencing, and it was anything but displeasure – quite the opposite. How could this be?! How was it possible that even with an unintelligible recording and bad acoustics, the alchemy of the Stillness Session had crossed all apparent barriers to touch the hearts of those listening?

The recording continued and when it ended, no one seemed to want to open their eyes. When they finally did, I knew something out of the ordinary had taken place. My cynical host asked if this experience would stay forever. He said he would do whatever it took to keep it alive. His attitude and behavior had completely shifted from night to day, from black to white.

the transcendence of unexpected gifts

The young American missionary opened his eyes slowly when the recording ended. He spoke of the experience as one of deep tranquility. He was at once thoughtful and then quite animated as he spoke of his life passion to make a difference in people's lives: "I want to create solutions for making this a better world." His words were colored by the enthusiasm of a visionary speaking the dream of his future into existence. "I believe it's possible. I just don't think people ever really hear each other anymore."

During the rest of the time we spent together he didn't speak of anything that created a divide between him and our host. Anything that might have caused separation, such as religion, culture or beliefs, melted in the space of pure presence. All that was left for this trailblazer of a new world to share, was the kindred light of his own heart.

The missionary from Polynesia had the look of someone who has just seen the true wonders within ... and is left speechless. I know that look; it's when you have no words to describe the colors that now flood your world with new sensations and feelings. I asked my host to translate.

"Can you speak English?"

"Only very little."

"Did you understand what I said on the CD?"

"Only very little."

"Something happened, didn't it?" The experience hadn't left him. The dark-skinned missionary, who looked like an athlete with his massive build, had the most tender look on his face. And even though he spoke in a language that was unknown to me, I could *feel* everything he was sharing.

"My mind became very still. Suddenly, there was so much light … And, It was coming from *inside me* … and going out from me to the entire world …" Silence overtook him once again. What is there to say, when you first come to know that you are so much more than you ever imagined?

the invisible reality of now

Each one of us, on the windswept deck that was now flooded with the sun's shimmering rays, learned something that transformed our view of the world. I discovered how the subtle energies of consciousness imprinted on the recording didn't need music or any descriptive content to transmit what profoundly impacted each person's life. Tamahere would discover in the coming days, hidden traumas from childhood that released him from a lifetime of pain,[1] and both of the young missionaries gained access to the innate wisdom that would enlighten their future.

The confluence of this moment was ingenious; of each person whose life would be forever changed, from an indefinable experience, offered by an acoustically challenged recording. What could orchestrate a symphony of this magnitude? The smile on the photographer's face matched the awe in her voice; she had traveled to every continent throughout her illustrious career, had seen the world's greatest wonders, and this day was now high on her list of unimaginable adventures.

The journey ahead promises untold wonders for each of us when we are open to experience this invisible world ... one that elevates our innate intelligence, heals emotional trauma and inspires the future. Even the sun-kissed shores of Tahiti pale in comparison to what we can learn ... although I would certainly return at anytime, to this amazing lab of dreams.

epilogue

In the days ahead, that illuminating experience continued to accelerate Tamahere's passion for life; the Energy of intelligence grew within him quite naturally, and he continued doing Stillness Sessions to further integrate it. I traveled to a neighboring island for a few days, and when I saw Tamahere on my return, the deep lines on his face had melted, and a happy, you could even say joyous, man had taken his place. Something had shifted.

Light was, literally and figuratively, shining through the dense matter of his body and radiating happiness on his face that everyone within a wide radius of him could see. Trauma from his past had surfaced,[2] and now he was reflecting just how luminous we are when blocked cellular memories are released.

The harmonic convergence of what exists beyond the sounds we hear is the unstruck chord of life; it is a gift for each of us to recognize our true inheritance. Our mind and body can be in greater harmony, creating coherence with the natural flow of life. What I learned on that day astounded me. The *subtle energies* imprinted on the *scratchy* recording weren't actually using (musical) electromagnetic sound waves. This advanced energetic intelligence couples on carrier instruments to flood your entire mind and body with its brilliance. It's like getting caught in a downpour of rain, where you get washed clean just standing in it.

Now might be the best time for you, to just take a moment and become immersed in this exquisite shower of Love. After all, within moments, you could end up in Tahiti ... and, on those beautiful sun-kissed shores ...

And, oh, by the way, when I next played that Stillness Session recording – it sounded perfect.

ACCESSING ADVANCED INTELLIGENCE

The ultimate wish for billions of people on this planet is to have peace of mind and the knowledge to live from your highest potential. Deeply sought throughout history, this knowledge has appeared as a distant dream, difficult if not impossible to attain. The 'belief' most of us have, i.e. what we've been told, is that the only way to access these miraculous treasures of life is through meditation, by having a calm mind or one that is completely devoid of thought. It's time to revisit this conversation and see if this statement is still true.

Meditation is definitely one way in, but it is not the only way. Meditation is not the goal, it is a helpful tool to access a dimension of indefinable Love, of infinite intelligence. There are many people today, more than ever before, who've had occasions of heightened clarity – but couldn't repeat it because they didn't know how to break through to that exquisite experience again. This is true for many people on a longtime journey as well, who have stopped trying to find this inner frontier.

Could there be simpler ways to access these desired states of advanced intelligence today? Since meditation is not an option for most people because, as we discussed earlier, for many it's dismissed as too time-consuming, boring or difficult – what else could be possible? While sages spent their lives and lifetimes in search of an enlightened state, most people aren't looking for that today – and if you are, you could still have the everyday constraints of dealing with financial challenges, finding a vocation that matches your dreams, or a relationship that brings more love into your life. So, what would inspire *your* journey – whether it's to understand the depth of your existence or to simply enjoy life? Anytime you narrow your focus, it supports your vision to become a reality. Let's do that now:

What do I want? I want to truly love my life and I want a practice that actives this experience. (If this vision doesn't work for you, please create another one.)

How would it work? It needs to be simple and easy to use, so powerful it rapidly increases joy and passion in my life and so enjoyable I want to use it.

How would it impact my life? It would 1) naturally eliminate my bad habits, 2) continually offer me insight and guidance, 3) inspire my life to be filled with love, inspiration, passion and fulfillment.

What would this practice look like (if not meditation)? And what would it do? Beautiful music and word recordings that I can listen to any time, and from wherever I am that activate creativity, vitality, healing and inner peace.

I wouldn't have believed this was possible at one time, and now I know it's true. We can access advanced intelligence – in new ways today through energetic tools and technology that *include* meditation, but are not reliant on it solely to elevate consciousness. Considering the capabilities of subtle energies makes it clear how this dimension can use various formats to offer the remarkable benefits that are occurring in people's lives today.

opening to evolutionary possibility

What I have witnessed in over a decade of research, has shown me unequivocally that what you connect with from this unified field, resonating through various catalysts, people, devices and technology, can completely redefine your understanding as it did mine.

Similar to the groundbreaking discoveries in science that are debunking beliefs we have held for so long, it's time to open to new discoveries that can assist us in connecting to higher levels of consciousness. This recognition will gain significant acceptance in the years to come as *you* magnify it in your life, and bring more people in the world around you to evidence it in theirs.

dissolving outdated beliefs

The time once required to attain deep peace and higher consciousness is a constraint we no longer need to believe in. Anyone can ignite this dynamic experiential process simply by listening to a Stillness Session where that exquisite Energy field activates a continuum of *experiential knowing*.

The experiences and long-lasting transformation that have happened for people who applied this uniquely loving and powerful technology has offered a wide range of benefits, from having experiences of deep peace rarely known (*see Prelude*) to manifesting extraordinary prosperity (*see The Dropped Call, The Elusive Dream*) to physical healing (*see Step Over the Line, Wordless Insights*). For some it happened very quickly – *and* not everyone connected through a deep meditative experience, but through the various formats the Simplicity of Stillness offers.

Stillness Sessions Technology utilizes the latest research on DNA (*see Part 3*) that demonstrates how it can shift through the syntax of language and word vibrational frequencies. All Stillness Sessions incorporate this science. As you repeat the words in the Sacred Word and Elevate Sessions, the intelligent cells in your body listen and begin naturally and organically rewiring, releasing and healing your mind and body. As you shift the environment (*see Epigenetics*) within you and surrounding you, life offers you even more to smile about.

your life responds to a new rhythm

The more attuned you become to this new *environment*, the more you feel it like a rhythm pulsing through your body, especially when you are still. And it becomes easier to connect with the advanced life Energy that is your soul's inheritance, since you can add a Stillness Session recording to your day in as little as four minutes. It's like preparing the body for a marathon; as more of these subtle energy vibrations are increased within, the strength you gain prepares you for the 'long run'. It guides your daily decisions, and inspires your actions to align with your true purpose.

Simply adding any of the recordings offered initiates the healing that reduces anxiety, depression, stress and so much more. The experiential wisdom that arises becomes the grounding base of your life.

the energy sea of potential

Theoretical knowledge; studying, reading and learning about higher consciousness is beneficial, but what exists beyond this structured framework is what evolves your life. Stillness Sessions take you there *experientially*, by increasing that still place inside – until it appears. Even when it feels like rocket fuel, just adding a session a day invites that well of ultimate potentiality.

What is unique to this audio technology is that even though your mind doesn't have to become still to access this awareness, through repetition of the various formats many people have experienced that their mind eventually does become completely still. Then they feel motivated to include the Deep State Stillness meditation in their weekly practice.

To consistently connect and live each day from your highest potential is a choice we can all make. Invitations to listen to Stillness Sessions have been placed throughout the book to gently remind you how easy it can be to maintain a higher energetic connection throughout the day. Various 'setbacks' will always occur as we evolve, but the totality of this connection and the experiences it inspires contributes powerfully to bringing that vision into reality – to living a life you love. What you will find in this section is what inspired each person as they invited this intelligence into their lives.

Doors that were closed, suddenly opened, and the most mundane circumstances became timeless moments. This elegant force magnifies the capabilities we have to transform every area of life – and, what you'll discover in the days ahead will assist you in weaving this treasure into each day of yours.

DEATH & DYING,
FROM FEAR TO LOVE

Patricia spent her life in the service of others; she was a healing practitioner who tirelessly applied the ancient art she had learned to bring people into greater health. Since this kind and compassionate woman's focus was usually on other people's needs, what she hadn't fully realized was that she'd been living with an unconscious fear of death.

Her healing abilities had assisted me through a difficult stage in my life, now it was my time to give back, to smooth her life's journey in the best way I knew how. I invited Patricia to experience what the conscious Energy of life had designed for her by listening to a Stillness Session. She lay down, closed her eyes, and the music began to play. When the recording stopped, she remained completely still with her eyes closed. I imagined she wanted to stay in the state she had accessed, but when she didn't budge after ... 5 minutes ... then 10 ... then 20 ... I became a bit concerned.

I decided to observe Patricia more closely; she was a mature woman in her 80s who I had believed to be in a healthy condition. While her breathing had slowed down considerably – I was happily reassured by the fact that she *was* still breathing. I had never witnessed anyone who didn't come out of Stillness for this length of time. I called her name softly, again. No response. I wondered what I would learn from this unusual situation. When her eyes finally opened, she shared the experience that completely transformed her previous concerns. Patricia's hushed voice registered the rarity of knowing what exists just beyond the boundaries of this reality: "I wanted to stay there forever … It was so loving … and so beautiful … Now I know where I'm going – and I'm not afraid anymore."

Today, Patricia is in her 90s, loving her life and, as always, sharing that love through the care she offers others. How beautiful that she could experience for herself the infinite Love that releases the most human of all concerns. From the fear of dying – to acceptance of the road ahead – how truly divine is that.

INSIGHTS, QUESTIONS & REFLECTIONS

Can anyone release their fear of death? Patricia and people in the SOS Scientific Study (*see Appendix*) demonstrated that it's possible to have an experiential connection that releases the fear of death. The Stillness Session audio not only shifted an entrenched belief – but evidenced that it can happen *instantaneously*.

Does this mean other painful entrenched beliefs can also be released this rapidly? It's possible, and I have seen it happen more frequently over a period of time, as layers of unconscious patterns are unlocked, physiologically and psychologically within the body and mind.

Since the mind often relaxes when listening to calming music, this energetic information coupled on sound is a simple way to eliminate fears. Considering the DNA study (Part 3), higher frequencies imprinted on the words spoken in the recording can assist with shifting limiting patterns. As discussed earlier, not all music or words will have this same effect; in fact, some could have the opposite as highlighted in the well-known research of Dr. Masaru Emoto on water crystals.[1]

Would listening to the Stillness Sessions Technology assist all people going through *transition* to have a similar experience? The Energy field transmitted through these recordings activates the higher consciousness in you, which brings experiences of inner peace and has helped many. But will everyone have a similar experience? Probably not – as we all evolve differently. Any easing of fears related to dying is certainly helpful.

This is where the practice of adding Stillness Sessions daily can become an ongoing support. People often play them in hospitals to assist others going through various challenges.

REFLECTION: How could change in a belief happen so rapidly? And, what could cause it to be life-lasting?

Anytime you want to invite answers from the deep knowing in you, go into the Stillness where all questions are resolved. Suggestion: Try a Deep State Stillness Session for this Reflection:

Close your eyes …

Listen …

Let the world slip away …

POWERLESS TO POWERFUL: KATIE & THE BULLIES

Big brown eyes, framed by big black glasses, a tiny heart-shaped face, and the sad countenance of one who has seen too much pain in a short-lived life. Katie said hello in a very grown-up manner, offering her hand in greeting, but without the usual smile you find when being introduced to someone for the first time. Her mother's entreaty to help her ten-year-old touched me deeply. The young girl's father had died suddenly of cancer, and the ravages of that malevolent disease had left his daughter and wife to confront a world without the security and love of the most important man in it.

Katie's eyes reflected the emptiness she felt. She was isolating at school, her grades were dropping, and she didn't have and didn't want any friends. We sat together on the floor. I asked her to breathe with me, to close her eyes and allow that soothing wave of deep peace to ignite within. The time in Stillness was brief. Five, six, seven minutes as that Energy of consciousness streaming through the recording unlocked the gates where Katie had stored her broken heart.

She spoke very matter-of-factly about how she could use what she had just experienced, "Sometimes kids do things at school and everyone laughs ... and I don't want to. If I do *this*, I won't have to join them." Katie was talking about the mocking and bullying at school. The peer pressure was evidently so intense that it was hard not to join in. Now she'd found the perfect practice to give her strength so she wouldn't have to participate. And so began the magical journey of a ten-year-old who clarified for all to see just how easily a child can assimilate their true power, and transform the world in which they live.

I didn't see Katie for over a year. She continued listening to Stillness Sessions, often two to three times a week before going to sleep. She put them on her media player and would drift into whatever world they opened. Life began to shift for this shy, retiring young girl in ways that even her mother didn't predict. Getting a role in the school play put her out in front despite her previous notions of wanting to hide, and she made new friends with a wide range of people, including the teachers who enjoyed hearing her unique perspective on life. From world events to everyday issues, this newly outspoken child always seemed to have something insightful to add.

The day began much like any other, but it was the day Katie would meet with providence in a crowded hallway at school. Susan was 5ft, 7in tall, and while this height might offer incredible possibilities in future years, in third grade it often meant she was made fun of and humiliated. Today, that abuse escalated; a group of boys surrounded her, inflicting their schoolmate with the cruelest and most dehumanizing jokes they could think of.

The head bully was taunting Susan with his cell phone, telling her how *utterly ridiculous* she looked, and how many people would laugh when he posted her photo on Facebook.

Backed into a corner feeling mortified, frightened and helpless, with nowhere to turn, the young girl joined the many who hold these memories as indicators of their future. Only now, all Susan wanted to do was to make it go away: not only the bullies, but that demeaning feeling inside her – she just wanted to make it all go away.

Katie's inner strength had grown exponentially in the last months; acting from the core of self-worth she had found, she walked directly into the circle of bullies. "Stop it! Just stop it!" she demanded. The lead bully shouted back. Katie grabbed the girl, and took off for the principal's office. She'd had enough of his *meanness* – it just had to stop, and today was the day!

Simple acts of courage can have a lifelong effect on many people's lives – this was one of them. Katie soon recognized the power she had to make a difference in the lives of others; the parents who came to school to discuss the incident realized that even kids from nice families can have issues and need to look closely at what else they can do for their own kids. The bully never mistreated anyone at school during the rest of his time there, and the tall young girl sidestepped what could have been a more traumatic memory if her image had landed on Facebook as they had threatened.

What could possibly have happened in the life of this little girl with big glasses that took her from being a shy, isolated child, to being a catalyst for change? She never thought of herself as a hero; she was just doing what came naturally. People often think they'll be weakened by the innate power of Love, not realizing it is their true potential. They think they will become vulnerable and not have the strength to stand up for themselves or what they believe in. Just the opposite is true. Courage, commitment, caring and engaging in life is what inspires Katie – and what she now teaches others is how to find it within themselves.

INSIGHTS, QUESTIONS & REFLECTIONS

What gave Katie the courage to do what she did? Parents of children who were bullied often report that no one, no child or teacher, ever spoke up about the mistreatment of their son or daughter – until it was too late, and they had taken their own life. Katie's self-worth had skyrocketed as well as her values. The fact that she responded in the face of any fears she might have had, demonstrates what happens when connecting to higher consciousness. She had greater courage and strength, and her connection to higher awareness inspired the insight for the actions she took.

Katie's actions open a new possibility. A child will stand up for another when they have found what is of inherent value within *them*. Katie continues to work with kids being bullied today.

Do painful memories of being bullied affect a person's future? Your *environment,* the thoughts you think, have a powerful effect on your entire life. Now, through what we are learning from epigenetics (*see Part 3*), these memories can even be carried forward, into the next generation.

Can a person *forget* a traumatic incident(s)? I have worked with many people, teens and adults, who speak of having been bullied or abused as a child as well as those who have other traumatic memories. These memories color their daily decisions years into the future. It affects what they believe about their potential, their ability to be loved, and countless issues that play repeated self-defeating thoughts in the mind.

This is where synaptic pruning is important (*see Neuroplasticity*). As experiences of empowerment occur, it rewires your brain. New behavior and actions generate an entirely different future. And while the memory might not be forgotten, it won't trigger the same responses or have the same adverse effects on their health.

Is it important to treat the bully as well as the victim? Understanding the epigenetic *environment* of the bully, from the past to their present is equally important. Dr. Gabor Mate writes in *In the Realm of Hungry Ghosts*, "… the dynamics of bullying or victimhood are rooted deep in a wounded child's psyche."[1] "Behind every look, every word, each violent act or disenchanted gesture is a history of anguish and degradation …" What he witnessed in his research with addiction, he found to be similar with problems of bullying. My father was bullied and badly mistreated by his alcoholic father, and he later treated his children in a similar manner. If we don't treat the bully, the cycle will continue.

What can be done? Dr. Mate believes that a program aimed at changing or preventing behaviors fails if it does not address the psychological dynamics that drive the behavior in question. I only have to look into my own past to see that behavioral change is not easy. And, what this Energy field of awareness demonstrates unequivocally is that even entrenched patterns can shift.

STILLNESS SESSIONS
why, when, what & how

Activating advanced life Energy is an essential element for accessing your highest potential. The energetic dynamic in Stillness Sessions Technology heals limiting patterns, activates advanced intelligence, and expands immense love and power in you.

Listening to Stillness Session recordings rapidly accesses deep peace and your creative potential. This scientifically researched technology transmits advanced life Energy (subtle energies) coupled on waves of sound. Each time you listen to the music and words, you find more joy arising in your life.

Why is Stillness Sessions Technology important to me?
- **Increases** mental clarity, creativity, and vitality
- **Accelerates** deep peace, and an inner state of calm
- **Releases** emotional trauma and unconscious habits
- **Connects** you to infinite intelligence
- **Harmonizes** energetic fields in body, releasing cellular blocks, creating better health and wellbeing
- **Maintains** higher consciousness throughout the day and more ...

When do I apply it?
Bringing higher awareness into the practical of every day – your work, social and family life – is key. Consistently maintaining a higher energetic connection throughout the

day expands your consciousness, guiding you into inspiration with just a breath, eyes open or closed. Stillness Sessions can be added to an existing meditative program, or can become your core connection practice. Stillness Sessions are included with each SOS Tool to increase its potency.

What will I experience in Stillness Sessions?
Feeling calm, very relaxed or deep inner peace is reported by 96.5 percent of people – what is experienced in the moment is not indicative of the (subconscious, etheric or physical) healing taking place. People's experiences include:
- Sensations of pure love
- Visions of brilliant light, or colors, and symbols
- Physical sensations of heat, cold or pulsating energy
- Visions of people who have passed on or future intentions
- Mental chatter that can often bring insight

Keep it simple. By using the various processes, from Deep State Stillness to Sacred Word repetition, you are sending healing frequencies of advanced 'information' into your body's cellular structure and through your brain's neural pathways to set new patterns and override unconscious habits from the past.

STILLNESS SESSION FORMATS
Stillness Session recordings were designed to offer various entry points to activate a flow of higher awareness in 4, 7, 11, 18 minutes and longer. Here is how to use them:
- **Deep State Stillness or Sacred Word Session:** Find a comfortable space where there will be no interruptions.

Lie down or sit with your hands gently placed in your lap, uncross your arms and legs. Close your eyes.

- **Elevate or Sacred Word Session:** Take a walk or find a place at work where you can be by yourself. Practice while seated in a plane or riding in a subway. You can listen, or repeat the words silently or aloud.

- **DNA Healing Session:** Various recordings can be played as 'background music' throughout your day. Others can be used similar to Deep State Stillness.

I will be inviting you to return to Stillness consistently throughout the book to continually deepen your connection. I hope you will discover, as so many have, that the rewards of making this a consistent practice in your life are as immeasurable as they are pleasurable.

SOS TECHNOLOGY: STILLNESS SESSIONS

It can be as simple as – put on headphones and hit play.

Choose a Stillness Session best suited to your situation and environment.

- **Breathe deeply and release expectations**

- **Relax,** allow the experience to happen naturally.

- **Repeat** Session, play twice, or as needed to continue to elevate your energetic base level or to go deeper into Stillness.

After the Session:

- **Reflect**. Become aware of any shift in your base vibration, the release of tension and anxiety, and/or acceleration of peace and intuitive insight.

- **Write** inspired messages, now or in the weeks ahead. (Inspired messages detailed in Expanding Intuitive Abilities.)

now is that perfect time …

Close your eyes …

Listen …

Let the world drift away …

JUST FOR YOU
STILLNESS SESSION TECHNOLOGY

Stillness Sessions are newly developed technology that transmits a vital life energy on carrier waves of sound. These scientifically researched audio recordings of beautiful music and words activate deep peace and the flow of higher awareness.

www.theSOSmethod.com/sos3audios

SCAN QR CODE TO PLAY AUDIO
Special Tip: For ease of access put your Stillness Sessions on your cell phone, ipad/kindle, & computer. For listening pleasure use headphones.

To access this material you will need to enter the following code when you reach the page. Code: U2KOE1LS

Deep State Stillness

Breathe... Just Breathe

18:23

Sacred Word Session

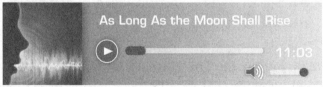

As Long As the Moon Shall Rise

11:03

Elevate Session

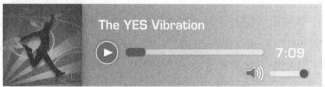

The YES Vibration

7:09

If you would prefer to receive your Stillness Sessions on a CD, simply visit the website above and select the "get a CD" option.

THE THREE BREATH AWARENESS
why, when, what & how

The Three Breath Awareness is a tool for *reconnecting* to the peace and higher awareness activated in Stillness Sessions. It's like a gateway for bringing this power instantly into your everyday life. Time slows down as you connect to a deeper sense of tranquility and wellbeing. You discover an ability to readily access the clarity and insight from higher intelligence to make better decisions

Why is the Three Breath Awareness important to me?
Most people think they can't acquire or maintain a connection to this potential because of their busy lives. With the Three Breath Awareness, you'll find that concept being broken. It isn't only about having time for lengthy meditations, it's about having access to higher intelligence throughout the day – eyes open or closed.

When do I apply the Three Breath Awareness?
Apply this SOS Reconnection Tool anytime you need to slow life down, or simply want to activate the field of awareness where better solutions are created. Also when going through difficulties of any kind, as it immediately improves your state of mind and upgrades the outcomes you are looking for.

What makes Three Breath Awareness different?

It's not just about breathing. And it's not just about taking deep yogic breaths. It's about attuning to advanced conscious Energy at all times, weaving it throughout your entire day. Once you have integrated this life force, you will be able to reconnect simply by returning to the breath with an inward focus – regardless of what is happening in your moment-by-moment reality. Once you access this power to align with your highest potential, you'll want to return again and again.

SPECIAL TIP: The level of stress you were in will determine the breaths needed. In time you will be able to access this shift in consciousness in only a breath. This process can be done with your eyes open or closed. Practice initially with your eyes closed until you are able to reconnect within a few breaths.

SOS RECONNECTION TOOL: THE THREE BREATH AWARENESS

1 APPLY: REFLECT, take a moment to become present.

   a. **Close your eyes or find a point of focus**. You can be standing or sitting in a crowded situation or by yourself.

   b. **Begin breathing VERY DEEPLY.** Breathe so deep you feel the air moving throughout every cell in your body, from the top of your head to your toes.

   c. **Feel any tension in your body releasing** with each breath.

   d. **Follow your breath inward**, away from the distractions of the outside world toward that deep well of serenity. Feel everything slowing down …

2 ACTIVATE: THE ENERGY POTENTIAL DEEPER WITH EACH BREATH. Maintain this inner focus for three minutes or longer.

3 ACT: FROM THE INSPIRATION AS IT APPEARS.

   a. **With your eyes closed**, notice how you feel, what has changed. Many speak of a renewed feeling of calm.

   b. **Open your eyes** and bring the Stillness awareness and higher vibration back with you into your day.

SPECIAL TIP: This is a Tool to be used *after* you have practiced the Stillness Session Technology. It's like an anchor; you feel the Energy stream re-ignite and in just a few breaths, you are back in connection. Your mind slows down, your body could feel the same tingling sensations, and you rapidly access inspiration and better solutions.

how daring have you been with your imagination

where do you let it play

with so many playgrounds in life

which ones will you choose

work, adventure, lovers, health, and wealth

dream all that you wish into being

only don't leave out

the most important of all

without which

none would have meaning …

to know love

to know Infinite Love..

Marlise Karlin

PART 5
TOOLS, TEACHINGS
& STORIES

TRAINING THE BRAIN
practical & energetically powerful tools

I recently decided to buy a new security system. When evaluating which would be best, my assistant and I noticed that we were attracted to those that offered the simplest procedures. Later, when studying the various components with the technician, it was evident that an enormous amount of complex information had gone into making this sophisticated system as user friendly and simplistic as it was. Because of its simplicity, it actually motivated us to use it. How often have you bought something or started a program, only to find you dropped it when it became complicated or it didn't fit easily into your life?

getting real, keeping it simple

I'm sure you get what I am leading up to. Simplicity is good, especially when it comes to interpreting incredibly complex information. Simplifying the science, as well as the depth of knowledge hidden within healing and wisdom traditions, has been my intention while writing this book. I readily admit it has not always been easy, and I have found that metaphors, images and stories often inform better than actual data, so I have included all of the above. What I know is, when you find something that is truly beneficial to your life, it needs to be simple to become a part of it, so it becomes *just the way you live*. If you enjoy it and it motivates you to use it – all the better.

narrowing your focus

You have approximately 60,000 thoughts in your head each day. Your mind is busy multitasking, thinking of a wide range of what and where and how it needs to do all that you do, to keep up with life's complexities. When you narrow that focus, which is what an SOS Tool does, and then activate your thoughts with the field of all potential resonating through the Stillness Sessions – your impact, influence and creative abilities skyrocket. This is where you see answers arriving before you even ask. SOS Tools also assist in calming your mind as you know that you will find solutions to whatever you are looking for – after all, when you are accessing the source of all potential – what isn't possible!?

SOS Tools are made to fit into your life just as it is. You don't need to spend hours a day practicing them, go to month-long retreats or wait years to see transformative benefits. SOS Tools eliminate the discord within your mind and body each time you use them. Soon, you respond to life in a way that brings enthusiasm to every situation. Reactions that caused stress and upset become a thing of the past. This dynamic interchange is another way to stream universal life intelligence through you, as each tool includes the use of the Stillness Session Technology. It becomes a part of you, like the hum of a high-performance vehicle.

training your brain

Since information from infinite intelligence requires a depth of understanding beyond our brain's usual thinking capacity, consciousness opens higher levels every time intelligent

Energy is activated. Dr. Ernest F. Pecci, M.D. defines how this changes the function of the brain.[1] "There is currently confusion between thinking and consciousness. Thinking is an autonomous activity of the brain, which, in most people, proceeds outside of conscious awareness and has little or no power to affect the environment, except as part of the general energy state of the individual.

"Conscious thinking toward the creation of a new thought pattern in order to shed new light on the solution of a perplexing problem is a much different matter.

"In a highly creative individual the brain must be trained to create new thinking channels … Ideally, these two processes, i.e., the acquisition of higher mental states and the training of the brain to access them, proceeds in harmonious tandem."

The New Science reviews how this energetic connection actually affects the brain to override old patterns by rewiring the neural pathways. As you act on the inspiration received, you discover new habits being set in place. Entrenched beliefs are difficult to change, and yet they are powerless in the face of higher consciousness. The more you voyage into illumined understanding by applying what you experientially learn, the easier it becomes to claim this potential that resonates openness, compassion and generosity.

from chaos to flow

It's so easy to get caught up in the chaos of life, to get triggered by the daily insanity that brings knee-jerk responses, resistance in all forms, and before you know it – depression, anger and confusion. There is a way out!

Believe me, I've been there. And the more you include these tools, the more you will feel the relief that happens when resistance dissipates and is replaced by happiness, optimism and clarity.

As we all know, habits take time to form. And, while many benefits appear immediately, there are some that can only happen over time. What you learn experientially from the Making Requests tool is that you no longer have to be in the re-active mode that worry sets in place – you know where to get answers. When you apply the Expanding Intuitive Abilities tool, your awareness accelerates and you discover how these abilities will make life so much more enjoyable. It is through your participation that you discover the extraordinary skills, talents and qualities you have, as well as the ability to release negative habits.

There are five SOS Tools included with this book that can be immediately applied to your life. It doesn't take long to see the results, they appear in a multitude of ways. Some might seem uncanny and all of them will begin shifting your perspective of what is possible for you. The SOS Tools included in this book are:

• **Release & Let Go:** eliminate blocks, generate new habits

• **Making Requests:** access knowledge and solutions

• **Expanding Intuitive Abilities:** accelerate capabilities beyond the mind

• **Transmitting Conscious Communication:** increase effectiveness through thinking, speaking, and transmitting

• **Setting Potent Intentions:** generate creative thought with potency

simple without powerful ... simply wouldn't work

It's wonderful to be able to calm the mind and relax – but is that enough? When you attune to higher consciousness you experience all of life becoming a creative flow. You will read about people from 10 to 90 from all cultures who discovered their lives becoming quite miraculous. The capabilities they realized can be drawn into your life as well. Here is just a sampling of what is possible for you:

- Hopefulness and loss of resistance
- New conscious habits forming
- Breakthrough in self-expression
- Physical health improvement
- Signs of mental and physical release
- Honest communication between family members
- More loving interpersonal relationships
- Relationship with self shifting, release of shame, blame, and anger

No matter what you do – simple is always good – and, if it's not combined with what is *powerful* the benefits won't be as effective. Powerful is good, but if it isn't *simple*, you might not embrace it.

Whether you are applying an SOS Tool, listening to a Stillness Session or taking a Course, you are nourishing, renewing and circulating greater harmony into your life and the lives of those you interact with. As you read the stories in this section, I hope it will not only inspire you but will entice you to make these tools a part of your life as well.

RELEASE & LET GO
eliminating blocks,
embracing new habits & beliefs

Your true potential and loving nature can be hidden from view when there are blocks within the mind and body. The stress, illnesses and many of the challenges you face today have roots in the past that are energetically imprinted in your cellular structure. True healing occurs when you can address these three important elements: mental, physical and emotional.

It's easier for new beliefs and habits to be established once this blockage in the body has been released *and* negative patterns in your neural pathways have been replaced. The cohesive Energy of infinite intelligence streams healing information through your directed focus in Release & Let Go to transform the overall quality of your life and bring greater love, strength, empathy and appreciation into each day.

ONE MAN'S CRY FOR LOVE

The epitome of the hardworking American middle-class, Gene was Irish American, 6ft 4in, 280lb, and every man's best friend. A religious man, he worked tirelessly to support his wife and family, laying deep tunnels throughout the Smoky Mountains, across Washington State, and along the East Coast. Life wasn't easy, but it certainly wasn't as hard as it became when he was diagnosed with ALS, the motor neuron disease also known as Lou Gehrig's unfortunate second claim to fame. Like an uncontrollable violent storm that overtakes its domain, each day the rampant disease eroded his ability to care for himself. The bitterness he felt clouded his mind. *Why? Why me?*

Gene's fury decimated anything in its path – he raged at everyone. He was angry! So very angry! At 15 months in, Gene was in need of a breathing machine and full support from caregivers. His resentment filled every corner of the house; tearing at the hearts of those he loved most.

Patsy knew how to deal with a big man's temper; after 44 years of marriage, this wasn't the first time she'd seen her husband angry, but this time it was different. It hurt. Much more than if she'd been sick herself. And while it was understandable, it made it almost impossible to care for him. Thank God, their daughter, Robyn, had returned home to do what she could to support them, but it was getting more difficult each day. In the first week of the SOS ALS Scientific Study (*see Appendix 1*) Robyn sent this plea for help: "I'm hoping that I can receive some encouragement and guidance on how to deal with anger issues. My father is so angry with everyone – and everything around him. I have tried talking to him but I can't seem to help him."

Nothing they did seemed to get through. I invited Robyn to play the Stillness Sessions aloud, so Gene could hear them. And then to follow through with that week's lesson as I felt it would guide her to the best answer. While I could have given her advice, what I have learned is that it's better to teach people by empowering them. The awareness that expands within when doing the practices will always give you the best answers. It didn't take long before she sent another note. Their healing journey had begun:

"My dad had a breakthrough, which felt so awesome. He said he was sorry for being so difficult for the past few weeks and that he was having a really hard time dealing with the disease. I gave him the biggest hug and told him I loved him and that I was sorry too – and that I will always be here for him no matter what. He has been open and calmer in the past week. I am *so* grateful!"

When the next call for the ALS participants came around, Gene was on it, and was speaking. Wow. He even made a few jokes with me on the call. It wasn't long before I got another note from Robyn; this time I got an inner message to call and speak with them all together as a family. They consented to sharing the transcript with you. The call was an hour in length, so it has been streamlined to highlight the most relevant elements:

Robyn:

He says he's enjoyed your sessions (Stillness Sessions) very, very much.

Marlise:

What do you feel from them?

Gene:

I feel just a lot of peace. (His speaking had gotten stronger in the past week and for the most part I was able to understand him.)

Patsy:

After the Forgiveness Session …[1] and, what he's talking about is that you can listen to it again, and again – and you do feel an inner peace. I did the crying thing – and when I knew he was asleep, I really got into it.

Marlise:

That's beautiful Patsy. My understanding is that everything that happens in life is to bring us closer to the recognition of who we truly are.

Gene:

I believe that.

Marlise:

Have you noticed when you're in that place of deep peace, that you're really not attached to your body at that time, are you?

Gene:
No, you're not.

Marlise:
So who you are is not your body.

Gene:
[Inaudible.]

Robyn:
He said no, you're something else – a soul or a spirit.

Marlise:
Exactly. And most of the time in life we are so outward-focused we are not taking even a moment to experience the spirit that we really are. And when we experience that spirit, it's so fulfilling, isn't it?

Gene:
Oh yes.

Patsy:
Because you wake up in a better frame of mind and just ready to meet the day. And it kind of makes you go, "I can handle this."

It felt like we had known each other for years. Patsy shared the deep sadness she was going through and Gene talked about his father who was an alcoholic and how he hadn't been able to forgive him. That he left his mother with five kids to take care of and life had been very hard for them. He said he never wanted to be like his father.

Marlise:
Sometimes people work hard to show their value. But you are of value just being you …

Gene:
[Inaudible.]

Robyn:
(speaking Gene's words) He said he's tried but he feels like he's let the Lord down a lot.

Marlise:
I think we all feel that way at some time, in some shape, or form. But that's where forgiveness comes in.

Robyn:
He said he's tried but he's failed.

Marlise:
What do you think you failed?

Gene:
Living for the Lord the way I should.

Marlise:
Do you know that every part of your life has happened in a way to guide you closer to your connection, truly to who you are as a child of God? So how can you fail? When your kids have made mistakes, did you love them less?

Gene and Patsy:
No.

Marlise:
You recognize that they needed to walk that journey to get more of their own confidence and value in life. So don't you think God wants that for you too?

Gene:
[Inaudible.]

Robyn:
(crying out …) But can't you just be enough? You've done the best that you could, and I love you for that, Dad. You've never failed me.

Gene:
I've failed to do the best.

Robyn:
You haven't by us.

Marlise:

(almost in a whisper) You know what Gene? This is good ... it's really perfect. You're expressing your pain. My guess is you haven't spoken about this very often.

Patsy and Gene:

No.

Marlise:

You're expressing what's really hurting inside you. And letting yourself down is the worst because there's nobody else to blame. So you put the blame on yourself. (Then I shared the story of what I went through in the experience where visions of my past made me feel ashamed.) The pain I felt was absolutely horrendous, I was on the floor weeping and crying because I felt I could never experience what I wanted – that place of pure love – because I didn't deserve it.

Gene:

I know the way you feel.

His voice reflected the penetrating sadness he felt. It was so moving, hearing this proud man share his deepest pain, allowing himself to be vulnerable in front of his wife and daughter. I wondered for a moment what it would have been like to hear my own father speak in this way, how it could have helped me understand, and love him more.

Marlise:

It's not easy to hear your husband be vulnerable, is it?

Patsy:

No.

Robyn:

This is the first time I've seen this from Dad. I've always seen Dad as the macho, big, brave, tough guy. This is the first time I've ever seen him in this light.

Marlise:

Makes you love him more, doesn't it?

Robyn:

Yes. I have so much love for you now, Dad … it's incredible … It's incredible …

epilogue

What could possibly break through all those social beliefs so many have to create this remarkable heartfelt experience for everyone in this family?

When I first spoke to Robyn and Patsy about Gene's anger and their inability to get through to him, I suggested it would be helpful if he could speak about the 'pink elephant' in the room, about his illness, and whatever he was going through. They said it was impossible, he was a 'macho' man and that he thought expressing yourself was 'feminine'.

The power of pure Love streaming through the method had burst through all apparent barriers, allowing Gene to release and let go of the anguish and fury he had carried for so long. This power heals what nothing else can. What better gift to receive in this lifetime ... than the depth of pure Love in yourself?

LETTING GO OF WHAT YOU DON'T WANT TO GET WHAT YOU DO

While there is an enormous power within you, living from your highest potential depends on your ability to let go of what doesn't serve you; whatever doesn't allow your innate brilliance to shine through. You can't experience the joy of being fully alive when you hold onto anything – whether it's the past, people or regrets of any kind. Intellectualizing what *isn't working* won't help. Neither will blaming life or others. As you let go of conditioning that has trapped you, a deeper truth begins to emerge.

Anytime you are in pain, feeling angry, overwhelmed, frustrated or even lethargic, recognize it as a signal that something in your life wants to change. When you feel those reactive triggers, which literally set off chemical reactions within your mind and body, you feel emotions that are uncomfortable. The impulse is often to look in the opposite direction, to blame outside influences.

In these moments we are far more likely to indulge our addictions, create drama in our relationships, or seek out distraction through other means. Although these diversions might help to pacify the moment, the chances that the feelings will be triggered repeatedly are increased, and you'll continue to re-experience them until they can be healed. You can *choose* to remain stuck in a static past, missing opportunities in the moment, or look deeper at what could be hidden that wants to be revealed.

forming conscious habits

Using these incidents to become aware of what blocks your connection to that loving stream of universal intelligence creates opportunities to heal the emotional cause of the pain. You don't need to be a professional or specialist to know that blocked emotions have innumerable negative impacts on your health. If you are listening, your body will always tell you when you're carrying emotional stress or negativity of any kind. Over time, through connection and integration of higher levels of consciousness, we become less inclined to remain in resistance of any kind, and it becomes easier to let go of old patterns and act from the new habits developed.

I discovered something wonderful as I began to do the process of Release & Let Go – it didn't take weeks and months of soul-searching, moaning and groaning over my inconsistencies and shortcomings. Simply by becoming *aware* of them, spending a bit of time in reflection, and then connecting to the power that eliminates the cellular memory where the pain is imprinted – works. As old patterns appeared, these tools and the audio technology assisted by replacing them with new conscious habits.

It's like taking a walk in the woods; there are moments where the trees block the light and it's dark, and then suddenly you are in a meadow, a clearing where there is nothing blocking the sunlight streaming in. There is so much joy and light that appears. Release & Let Go dissolved another old belief for me, that I had to suffer anytime I looked at an old pattern – it just isn't so. While you can choose to suffer, and some people do, letting go of this concept offers you laugh out loud happiness, sometimes mixed with a few tears, but always commingled with joy in your heart.

mental and physical go hand in hand

There are memories, generational and recent, stored in your subconscious and in the cellular structure of your body. This *environment* might have caused some of the challenges you face today (*see Epigenetics, Part 4*). The capacity to heal these mental, emotional and physical blocks is possible by shifting this dense matter into a higher frequency. Your body *can* recalibrate and get back into a natural flow.

It's important to understand that any limiting pattern, not brought into awareness, could and often does develop into illness. And, any cure or healing that occurs, whether through traditional or alternative health care, can revert back without an understanding of the mind-body connection – and how every element is important to the whole. It is coherency that brings about lasting change.

Various ancient forms of healing from Japan, China and India, concur that when dense emotional pain in the memory of our cells is released on physical and etheric levels, we are restored to our natural energetic body. I was always amazed how my body went through a physical cleansing of sorts when releasing blocks of any kind, and how I always evidenced a healthier body once it had passed. Many Eastern traditional and ancient techniques speak of this purification, as it is part of the process of healing.[1]

As mentioned in *Part 1: Energy & Awareness*, human beings vibrate at different frequencies; the Energy field of consciousness, light and peace is a high vibration that can be integrated into our denser bodies naturally over time. It doesn't happen all at once.

turning points

We are always evolving. Regardless of how much time you have spent elevating your consciousness, there is always another layer of illusion to be released that brings light-heartedness, appreciation, acceptance, and a new depth of awareness into your life. Our higher selves actually search for these turning points to literally *inspire* us into doing whatever it takes to move into the next chapter of our personal evolution. Many people find they suddenly choose healthier foods to eat, no longer drink excessive amounts of alcohol, and want to surround themselves with happier, more loving and kind people.

This voyage of discovery is designed to open your life to a spectrum of experiences you might not have dreamed possible before now. From becoming aware of restrictive beliefs and patterns, to clearing out excess baggage wherever you find it – all to make space for a new dimension of love and prosperity to enter your life. The more frequently you practice Release & Let Go, the phenomenal healing and outcomes you are searching for will be reflected in the peace and extraordinary potential you have realized.

WHAT YOU DON'T KNOW *CAN* HURT YOU

Like a volcano spewing molten ash, words poured forth claiming what she believed was an inherent right … to be right. No black, no gray, just bright white – right. The act of listening to another perspective appeared to be just that – an act. I knew it wasn't intentional; it's just what happens when a person's mental and emotional faculties are set up in a way that even the possibility of not being *right* can appear so painful, they will do anything to assert their point of view. Only then, it's not really a point of view, is it? *It's just the way it is*.

Regardless of what I expressed, it didn't seem to be heard. When a person appears adamantly opposed to what you have to say, the best recourse would normally be to invite them to look elsewhere for what they are searching for. But Jeannie Marie was committed to the process, and so I was committed to her. Usually the Energy stream resonating through the program breaks through a person's resistance long before any words I speak, but this was proving to be a unique situation. So, I continued searching for ways to uncover what those blocks were that had her, more often than not, relating from the anger erupting inside.

I knew her heart was loving, compassionate and kind; I just wasn't clear what had made the walls around it so impenetrable. As a caregiver Jeannie Marie gave of herself wholeheartedly, and maybe just a bit too much, as she placed her own wellbeing far behind everyone else's. After the first call I sensed that whatever was going on was buried deep.

Were her motives good? Yes. Did they come from wanting to fill a hole in her past? I imagined they did, and I knew the weeks ahead in the study, as the method continued to activate her healing process, would tell the tale.

As I contemplated what that next step would be, and if there was any, beyond allowing the process to unfold, a note arrived, not formed by the *spewing volcano*, but more from the pain that caused the constant eruptions. Before I could even ask, the first layer of answers arrived:

"I am so angry and so sad. I want to cry non-stop and scream 'RA-RA-RA' at almost everyone. I don't understand me ... I am trying so hard to do everything right ... because as a little girl that is what I learned I had to do if I wanted to be loved by my father and not to be yelled at or hit by him. This constant need to do everything perfectly and correctly has been my entire life. It has made me excel in school and work, but not in my relationships with people.

"Of course, no matter how smart I am and how perfectly I do anything, my father is who he is. When I was just a little girl after my parents divorced, my dad told me he was remarrying and that I would no longer be his little baby because he was having one with his new wife. So I feel like I have to do everything just right – and even then I'll still be replaced."

How many words have been spoken by an unconscious parent that ring as truth to the child throughout their adult life? I knew this kind of suffering all too well, and I knew that she had the strength to deal with it, otherwise it wouldn't have risen into her awareness. I encouraged her to look at the effect these words, spoken years ago, still had on her, and to continue doing the method as it would increase her strength and assist in setting new habits where she could feel more joy.

On the next call I assured her again of this progression, Jeannie Marie's response was like a mother bear protecting her lair, only what she was protecting was her right to be right, *and* to be angry. In the weeks ahead, each call included more of the same. The night before my final conversation with Jeannie Marie, I did what I always do, when I don't know what to do – I Made a Request and invited universal intelligence to bring me an answer. There was nothing immediately forthcoming, so I turned on my computer to find a film or documentary to watch, and to just relax.

I don't know exactly how I landed on this film, or why it caught my attention, but it was about an illness I had never heard of. As I watched a social anxiety disorder documentary: *Afraid of People*,[1] light bulbs went off in my head. Many of the symptoms people had in the film seemed to relate to Jeannie Marie – *and to me*. The symptoms I had as a child, and as an adult were not as severe as those depicted in the film, but it revealed how neurochemistry would fire off in the brain resulting in high levels of anxiety. I had lived with that sense of the world closing in around you, the fears of having to do even simple things publicly. I was forced to do things that frightened me, even things that other people never had a problem with – like asking for something at the store, or just playing baseball – and it made me so angry. I actually hid from gym for an entire semester because I was so afraid of looking like a fool when I got up to bat.

Silent tears began streaming down my face; a piece of the puzzle of my own childhood had just fallen into place. I sensed that somehow this also related to Jeannie Marie. The puzzle in her life was about to unravel on the call I made the next day:

Marlise:
You're learning so much. So the next level for you to notice is when you're feeling triggered – is it physical as well?

Jeannie Marie:
I *am* more aware of the things that bother me now … and how they affect me, and how they influence me, and how I'm dealing with them. I'm *aware* of all of it – but I can't change. I don't know how.

Marlise:
Over time, things will shift. The awareness you have is already so much greater. Your father gave you a lot of reasons to be in confusion and doubt, right? How he spoke to you has repeated in your head for many, many years. And that is not going to dissipate instantly. It can take time. We all get triggered and, when we do, old stuff just comes rising to the top.

Jeannie Marie:
That's the thing – I know it's happening, I can feel it happening, and I can't stop it. I get so anxious that I literally can't relax. My body can't relax; my mind can't relax. And then something happens that I should be able to cope with, but

because I've been in such a nervous state for so long, I can't cope. I freak out.

Marlise:

I hear you. I've got something to tell you. Last night I'm on the Internet, and for some reason, I end up on a YouTube video about a disorder called Social Anxiety. I don't know that you have this, but I found it really interesting from the point of view that it showed people who had anxiety so intensely that they couldn't deal with life normally. Sometimes it even got to where they had difficulty working, and communicating with people.

And then scientists discovered that some people have a bias to certain stimuli and it causes chemicals to shoot off in the body. And, after time, the body gets used to being in an anxious state. So it doesn't have the reserves of what to do in a calm way because it's so used to being in this highly anxious state. The hormones that help you calm down ... well suddenly they get shut off. And so you don't have the ability to access behavior where you're not anxious. It's just a theory, but I am wondering about your parents and what their life was like before you were born. Can you tell me anything about them?

Jeannie Marie:

Yeah, my dad has anger issues and my mom has a generalized anxiety disorder. And, I have the best of both of them. [Laughs]

Now, I understood why the volcano continually erupted. What she shared reminded me of the study where the offspring of that mother with high levels of anxiety (*see Epigenetics*) carried that hormonal imbalance in future generations.

This could be what caused Jeannie Marie to consistently react to people in the way she did. It is also the best reason I can think of for why it doesn't make sense to get upset with people when they don't respond in the way you wish they would. If you look into the past, the windows of a person's world give you so many reasons to have compassion. What developed the behavior they display? The next part of her story opened my eyes even wider.

Jeannie Marie:
When my mom was pregnant with me, they bought this house – it's the house that my mom and I both live in now. As soon as they moved in, my dad went nuts and he started punching holes through all the walls in our house. And my mom was like, "Oh my God. What is going on!?" So she called his sister and said, "Do you know about this? Has he ever done this before?" And his sister was like, "Yeah, he used to do it all the time in Venezuela." And that's when she was pregnant with me.

Marlise:
So she must have been frightened as well as anxious. What about your father?

Jeannie Marie:

He told my mom he was going take us to Venezuela and she couldn't get us back. And so she had to stay with him. And there was a lot of domestic violence in the house.

Marlise:

One thing for you to notice, is that the man she married wasn't the same person who showed up later. Maybe this will help you to stop blaming her. But the bottom line is, all this anxiety in your mother could have gotten passed down to you. And what you're doing right now is becoming aware of it so you can move beyond the pattern. And that doesn't usually happen overnight.

Jeannie Marie:

I have to tell you, when I did the Stillness Sessions maybe a couple of hours a day, it felt *really good*! But I can't do that every day, a couple of hours a day.

But, what's really interesting, I was talking to my friend and she said, "... you're really negative, and you're being really mean to me." And I was like, "What?" I think the real point is, she was a messenger for me. Like, "You're not sensitive to how your words affect other people."

Marlise:

Wow ... you are looking at things that could be so painful, that you would never have looked at before. And now you have this beautiful sensitivity of, "What can I learn from this?" You're not blaming your friend and making her wrong, you're looking at her and asking, "Is there something I can learn from this?"

Jeannie Marie:
Yeah. It's true ... And, I can be a nasty person when I choose to be.

Marlise:
And you can be an amazing, loving person when you choose to be, as well.

Jeannie Marie:
Yeah. I've just got to let that other stuff go ...

There was a crack in the window of Jeannie Marie's reality. The light of awareness was shining brighter than ever. Would the volcano stop spewing? Probably not right away, but the more her ability to see clearly expands she will know what to release, and can continue letting go of her resistance as well. I believe her journey to truly heal was now fully underway. How very fortunate for her and the children she might birth one day, who won't have to carry this pain she has known, into their future as well.

INSIGHTS, QUESTIONS & REFLECTIONS

If a person has a "temperamental bias" to certain stimuli that results in reactive behavior,[2] are there ways to heal these chemical reactions naturally? Ana had a variety of challenges, including anxiety disorder (although I initially didn't realize it) (see *Finding Your Truth*). In later years she didn't have any of the symptoms associated with it. This is the first case of 'anxiety disorder' that I have knowingly worked with. As Mary Burmeister would say, many illnesses have *labels* that tend to frighten us. And yet, when given the right circumstances, natural healing can occur.[3]

Jeannie Marie expressed her feelings, coming from anger, and it propelled drama into her life. How would this have helped? It wouldn't. It's important to recognize when you are repressing your emotions, as this can lead to future illness. And, finding the best outlet where you can release emotional stress (and not on an unsuspecting party) is equally important.

Can just being conscious of triggers/old memory patterns that affect you physically help you in any way? Can they actually be eliminated or will you always have them? The body can still register anxiety, fear or shame, even when you consider yourself to be very conscious, as these cellular memories are deeply embedded. The more you connect to the healing power of unified Energy fields, the more your brain assists you by cycling new neural pathways (*see Neuroplasticity, Part 3*). Once more loving, good feelings get fired off, they'll start taking over, and the body won't instantly spark chemicals that cause emotional stress and angst.

Could Jeannie Marie heal if her past remained buried? I don't believe we have to dredge up the past and play it over and over – but, by being aware of it, we can make conscious choices of what steps to take to heal any pain it has caused. When conscious Energy enters your system it causes dormant conflicts to arise, allowing the transmissions to bring healing through the body and the mind. It also helps when recognizing an emotion that has arisen that doesn't feel like who you see yourself to be. That way you don't have to act on it and can instead choose more resourceful activities that will ultimately make life more enjoyable for you and for everyone around you.

Jeannie Marie stated that listening to the Stillness Sessions made her feel good, but that she wished she could do it more often to stay in that pleasurable state. What else can someone do who has this level of anxiety? Maintaining and developing that life force Energy in you, *and* embracing the tools that direct your focus builds with momentum through constant practice. You can also include physical exercise; working out, yoga, walking, etc., and body treatments that focus on removing blockage as well as good nutrition.

REFLECTION: What triggers you? Could it be something that might have been passed down to you?

Now might be the perfect time, to dive into that continuum of love and calm and inspiration by listening to the Deep State Stillness Session (*see Just For You Stillness Sessions Page, Part 4*). It's always the right time to feel good, to Release & Let Go!! All you have to do is …

Close your eyes …
 Listen …
  Let the world slip away …

WORDLESS INSIGHTS

A shock of white hair made him stand out even more than his towering height and commanding build. The image of the Marlboro man riding across a Western frontier came to mind, only the setting was a red brick building on the canals of Amsterdam. Evidently, a friend had insisted he come, yet there wasn't any resistance in his posture, rather a sense of total absorption as he quietly immersed himself in every element of information given.

It was a stormy winter day, rain cascaded down beyond the curtained windows of the cozy room where the retreat was held. Each day was a fusion of intoxicating information that revealed untold knowledge, with time spent in Stillness, where the aware presence emanating through the recordings offered captivating insights rarely experienced. Much like riding a horse heading out into *the wild yonder* – where anything is possible.

This could be the day for a wild ride on a bucking horse that doesn't want to be tamed, similar to the mind, or it could be the day for a gentle ride, similar to a caring embrace. Then again, you could find yourself on a runaway that takes you into mysterious surroundings where you are so in awe of what you see and feel, you want every second to last a lifetime. You never know what will transpire, until it does.

As the retreat came to a close, the Marlboro man whose name was Patrick spoke for the first time. It was in measured tones, as though he had to search for the words he now voiced:

"I have the impression that what has happened … is that I've been reconnected to something I was connected to when I came into this world …"

You could *feel* what he was trying to convey. It was like a force field, a sound wave that grew in strength as it rippled out from him to everyone in the space. There was a hush in the room as he concluded his thoughts:

"… and from now on … the strength of that connection will grow … It gives wordless insights ... I'm very happy." He smiled briefly and went back into the Stillness from where his words had arisen.

A year passed before I saw Patrick again: this time it was in Vienna, Austria. The crevices that had lined his face, revealing the stress of a hard-lived existence, had disappeared and were replaced by the look of a person who is okay with life, and inspired by its passage. Patrick spoke of the many changes that had transpired. He had been through a lot of rough terrain and the end result was that he had stopped drinking.

After *30 years* of consuming a quart of Jack Daniels whiskey every day – *he stopped drinking*. Patrick began having more of those *wordless insights* he had spoken of. Strength and courage emerged. It had now been seven months since he had taken his last drink. Life was changing. He said there was no turning back, and that he was ready to look even deeper into that mystical world that had so inspired him.

What could assist a man to completely halt an addiction after 30 years are the seemingly impossible and yet evidential markers of what is available to each of us when the time is right. Regardless of what resistance or addiction has taken you on a ride, when this energetic field ignites, a conscious awareness resonates through you on every level. Whatever pain has locked you in its overpowering grip must eventually surrender.

The breeze at dawn has secrets to tell you …
Don't go back to sleep
You must ask for what you really want
Don't go back to sleep
People are going back and forth
across the doorsill where the two worlds touch
The door is round and open
Don't go back to sleep.
~Rumi

When an energetic force of this magnitude colors your world as it did for Patrick, there is often nothing left to say. Wordless insights … the power of Love, the power of knowing who you truly are …

INSIGHTS, QUESTIONS & REFLECTIONS
Can anyone heal from life-long addiction? When the force of advanced life Energy streams through the cellular structure of the body – it changes the energetic field,

transforming blocked lower density (condensed imbalance) into coherence.[1] We all have levels of blockage; therefore, recovery will be different for each person.

While I have witnessed extraordinary healing over the years (*see Prelude*), without consistent integration of this healing Energy to eliminate density in the mind and the body, new challenges can appear, and the addiction can return (*see Rock n Roll, Drugs & Higher Learning*). Various healing traditions, such as Jin Shin Jyutsu (JSJ), and finely tuned healing practitioners open blocked energy meridians in the body, greatly assisting the process. Applying the SOS Technology and Tools activates consistent expansion and integration of new habits that support mental, emotional and physical healing – as well as clearing out the cellular memories that can cause the addiction.

Why will some people heal and others continue to struggle? Are there more lessons to learn from the struggle? Could the body recalibrate itself more rapidly in one person because there was less damage from traumatic memory, or traits that had been passed down? Or less childhood trauma? I had been smoking pot for 15 years when I first experienced a higher healing frequency – I stopped smoking it within 24 hours, and stopped doing cocaine within 30 days. It took me another seven years to quit cigarettes. Can you make sense of this? Are cigarettes more addictive than cocaine – or did I need to find the strength within myself to fully participate in this release? These are all good questions for each person to find answers within themselves.

Does 'willpower' have anything to do with it? There are many variables to consider. And, if there is a chemical imbalance – your mind and body are fighting each other, and it becomes more difficult, yet, not impossible. The drug program "Just say no" made absolutely no sense to me. That statement could not have been made by someone who understood chemical imbalance in the body *and* mind – and how it can derail you.

Your commitment to shift an addictive tendency is absolutely helpful; as you set your Intention and add the potency of the Energetic field, your ability to heal is greatly magnified. And, it is an individual journey.

What role does dopamine have to play in a person's ability to stop their drug/alcohol/etc. addiction? Dopamine is a neurotransmitter formed in the brain, which is essential for the healthy functioning of the central nervous system. Using addictive drugs floods the brain with dopamine – as much as five or ten times the level needed for motivation and for mental and physical energy. Dr. Gabor Mate, and Peter Levine, Ph.D, leading experts on addiction, have this to say:

"When this happens the brain's own mechanisms of dopamine secretion become lazy. They stop functioning at anywhere near full capacity, relying on the artificial boosters instead. Only long months of abstinence allow the intrinsic machinery of dopamine production to regenerate, and in the meantime the addict will experience extremes of physical and emotional exhaustion."[2]

The euphoric effect of drugs and alcohol plays a big role in their constant use – whether a person considers himself an addict or just a 'social user'. A former addict, who participated in SOS programs, wrote this theory based on personal experiences of the sensorial *high* he experienced from the Stillness Session recordings: "I believe Stillness Sessions increase the amount of dopamine in the brain, and that repeated use literally re-wires it, eliminating the need for drugs, or alcohol. It literally calmed my hyperactive brain."

When I first experienced this heightened Energy, it inspired me to stop doing drugs because this 'high' was so much better. This is our true nature – a 'heightened sensorial connectedness' where all the senses are 'alive'. Many people have had moments of this level of connection, but it doesn't last as our bodies are not ready to handle it energetically. As the blockage in our system is released – our natural production of dopamine will more than satisfy the addictive cravings so common in people throughout the world today.

Imagine living on a natural high. Is that possible? When you experience what exists at the depth of Stillness you recognize that it's not as distant as it might seem. There is a natural vitality that becomes second nature. The more we heal, the more readily we will access those 'wordless insights' and can begin to live from the state of true joy that resides within.

RELEASE & LET GO
why, when & how

Release & Let Go is a tool for self-healing that propels you to *let go* of beliefs, expectations, and mental and/or emotional blocks that cause you pain – and invites you to step boldly into a new future. What is causing your anger, addiction, illness or frustration is *preventing you* from living at your highest potential, and might have been passed down to you.

Why is Release & Let Go important to me?

Your ability to release restrictive patterns and replace them with an empowering quality could make a difference, not just in your life, but for generations to come. You will:

- **Release worries, doubts and fears** that you're not capable of transforming life's difficulties.
- **Become aware of the critical unconscious programming (belief)** that has driven your life choices.
- **Open to the dynamics of newfound inspiration** and wisdom to enter your life.

When do I apply Release & Let Go?

Feeling angry, overwhelmed, or frustrated are all clues that a limiting pattern has been triggered. Letting go of whatever is causing your suffering alters your behavior, and establishes new beliefs and habits. An ability to respond in new ways is exceedingly beneficial to your overall health and wellbeing. Hope, happiness and joy consistently expand as the pain from your past – recent and generational – is released.

SOS TOOL: RELEASE & LET GO

1 APPLY TOOL & TEACHING:

  a. **Explore**/review SOS Teaching.

  b. **Reflect with Three Breath Awareness** – where do you feel powerless? And how incredible could your life be without this block (feel-good quotient).

  c. **Write one Block & one New Habit**

    • **Block:** Where you feel like you have no choice. i.e. anger, jealousy, fear, frustration, depression, anxiety, etc.

    • **New Habit:** Envision your new quality, i.e. inner strength, passion, enthusiasm, courage, empathy. etc.

2 ACTIVATE ENERGY POTENTIAL THROUGH STILLNESS SESSIONS TECHNOLOGY:

  a. **Listen** and experience the peace and power conveyed, allow it to heal and strengthen your resolve. Use any **Deep State** or **Sacred Word Session.**

3 ACT ON INSPIRATION AS IT IS REVEALED:

  a. Your first step is not to *react*, instead release triggers by doing something physical, take a walk, run, etc.

  b. Messages and insights will appear to guide you, today or in the week ahead. Continue to activate inspiration from potential.

  c. Journal what happens – as it demonstrates how guided you are, assisting you to recognize the advantages of continually letting go.

Your focused attention on what you want to release that no longer serves you, opens space for what you truly love to enter your life. Allow the coming days and weeks to present you with even greater clarity. Remember, you don't have to let everything go at once, it's a journey, you have time.

Release & Let Go supports you to blaze a path of healing, trust and true self-expression so you can live your life with the optimism and happiness that is your birthright.

MAKING REQUESTS
amplifying insight, accessing knowledge

The ability to find inspired answers to *every* situation changes your relationship to life – what challenges you *and* what you are passionate about. From knowing what to do in a crisis, to developing ideas that transform the way people live, from finding the best possible job, to simply clarifying the next step to take.

Making Requests brings knowledge and events that impact your daily decisions by entraining a quantum field of information to coalesce with your point of focus. It is an elegantly simple approach for accessing an information highway that offers insight to derail your detrimental tendencies and develop your ability to flow with life.

Consistent use amplifies your access to inspired insight, where life becomes a playground you appreciate and enjoy more every day.

THE UNIVERSE'S BIG MISTAKE

I think we all have a fantasy of what it would be like to be a 'fly on the wall', to hear exactly what is said in certain situations, or maybe just to hear what people *really* say when no one is listening. Tony, a world-class athlete, diagnosed with ALS (amyotrophic lateral sclerosis) graciously consented to our having this opportunity. The transcript on these pages was taken from a call at the end of the eight-week program in the Scientific Study (*see Appendix*); it was the first time I spoke with him one on one.

You can always tell when a person is actually doing the SOS practices – or just saying they are – some things you just can't fake. There is a shift that is inevitable and what happens generates the uncommon events that arise. What Tony shares with all of us is an exquisite gift. He speaks not only of the recent and past events that rocked his world, but offers an inside look at his shortcomings, ones we can all relate to – and the insights he gained in this, the *perfect* unfolding of his life.

I feel a bit strange putting in the effusive comments he had about SOS, as it might seem they were prompted, but it was just the enthusiasm that appears in all our lives when a downhill cycle suddenly makes a big turn. This is how it played out when I asked Tony what I could do to help him:

Tony:
You have already helped me. How about that? Doing all your Sessions really worked for me – and a lot of things have come into my life, from feeling better, to relationships, to people contacting me after not talking to them *for years* – just by putting stuff down on paper. It was amazing what happened. It really was amazing. I feel better. I feel more energy.

I've had this thing [he doesn't like to call it ALS] for – you know – five years now. But the last few weeks have been really, really some good stuff, *over* the last two years. So I've got to thank you. Your program definitely works.

Marlise:
I'm happy to hear that. It's beautiful what you wrote in the letter about the different things that began happening [how several people suddenly appeared that he wanted to meet with, as well as an opportunity to get a truck he always wanted to buy]. It's that level of synchronicity that starts to happen. And, suddenly you go, "Oh my gosh. This is what it's like being in the flow of life."

Tony:
I'm not the type of guy that gets so excited about stuff like that, but like I said, I didn't talk to a guy for, I think, ten years. And he sends me an email right after I started thinking about him. I couldn't get ahold of him. I had no idea where he was. BOOM! The email pops in, "I hope everything's well with you." I said holy smokes! [This happened in the Lesson on Forgiveness, Tony had Made a Request, he had written

this man's name as someone he wanted to ask forgiveness of, and soon after doing the steps in this tool, this is what happened.]

"And it snowballed from there. It just got better and better. A woman that I hadn't talked to, we're talking now, having dinner, hanging out. It's wonderful. And that's with me *not reaching out* to these people. That's what's amazing.

Marlise:

It's like the universe orchestrates things beyond what we can understand. And that happens when you're getting more connected with your true self. So you clearly are integrating, that knowing inside you.

Tony:

Oh yeah, then I started thinking about soccer, and, all of a sudden all this stuff is flowing. Clubs want me to be – oh, what's the word they said? – an advisor to the boards of two different clubs! All because I said I want to get back in, that I'd love to be a part of this.

And before you know it, coaches are calling. I just got a call before you called ... said he wants me back on his board, they need my advice. Honestly, it's unbelievable. All when I started thinking about it in the last weeks. [Tony's focus coupled with the Energy potential in the practices, brought the answers he was looking for.] Yeah, it's amazing. And I hope it works for other people. That's what I hope.

Marlise:

You know what it is, Tony? Everybody has a different journey. And so everybody has to walk their own journey in their own time. [We then went into a discussion about *healing*, and how it's different for each person.]

Your body's been talking to you, Tony. It's giving you messages. What is it that you need to look at? And it might still be unconscious, but you might have started getting indicators like, "This is an area I want to look into deeper." Where is there any dysfunction? Where is there breakdown in your life? [At this point, I wanted him to reflect, not to blame himself, but just look to see where his body was telling him that something was blocked.]

Tony:

One big anger for me is, like I said, I played for the US Nationals [inaudible]. I was ranked number two in the country. And then I got hurt at age 18. So I think I've been carrying that anger and bitterness forever. And for whatever reason, it's very difficult for me to let go of that.

My whole life was torn apart, and then it was over. I don't think I ever got over it. So I think that was a lot of anger toward other people, jealousy toward other people doing bigger and better things – playing professional.

I could have played in Europe, and I got hurt. And it's just one of those things that gets ripped away and, "Is it my fault? Is it someone else's fault?" These are the angers that I've carried for the last – jeez, I'm 44, so I was 18 when I got hurt.

Marlise:

How did you get hurt?

Tony:

Indoor on turf. Ripped my knee apart.

Marlise:

So it wasn't even, quote, "somebody's fault".

Tony:

No. It was faulty turf. It certainly was an indoor standard that wasn't the best. Back then you didn't have the state of the art stuff they have today. So it was kind of slapped together, but I played it for years. And one day, that was it. The turf wasn't the best, and snap – my ligaments just tore.

Marlise:

That's painful ... And so then they let you go, right? Because you couldn't play?

Tony:

That was it ... you try to get back but the surgery – they were butchers back then. They had no idea what to do. My scar's got to be, I would say 8in long. I was trying to get back, and pulling hamstrings, and pulling muscles. I could play, but never at that level. I played in front of 80,000, 85,000 people. I played in the World Cup, and I was well on my way to bigger and better things.

So I think there's a lot of resentment and anger, and I've carried that. And I've realized through your program that, man, I'm still bitter. I'm just angry all the time. Who do I forgive? Do I forgive myself? It's very confusing because everything in my life was just ripped out from underneath me, all by one little injury.

Marlise:

But if there's this overview ... Who do you believe in, that makes this universe go round? What do you believe in?

Tony:

I just believe in energy. I believe in energy flow, that type of stuff. I believe there's spirit and energy out there – flow. I believe everyone's connected with everything that's going on.

Marlise:

Then, consider this – [I spoke about the different names given by people, and that regardless what name you might give it, God, Buddha, Source] that Energy form is this whole universe. What is the purpose of being here, if it isn't to be in connection to that form? And do you think that tearing your knee is something that happened *outside* of the spectrum of your journey to know yourself?

Did the universe make a mistake?

Tony:
Probably not.

Marlise:

When you think of the all-knowing, the all-knowing that's now putting into place all those people that are showing up in your life – for forgiveness and for love and so many things – that's the all-knowing. So did that all-knowing just make one mistake in Tony's life at age 18, but got everything else right? Think about it.

Tony:

No, you're right. It makes sense. Makes a lot of sense.

Marlise:

So let's go deeper ... go back to the Making Request Tool, "Guide me and show me. Help me dissolve this pain. If this was meant to be, what am I to learn from that? What am I to learn?"

Maybe you need to be exactly where you are right now, because of the difference you're going to make in other people's lives. You could have gotten mangled on the field. Yes, you would have had the fame, and you would have had this and that, but look how many people have fame and they're messed up.

Tony:

Yeah, you just opened my eyes big time.

Marlise:

So walk the journey. Go into the forgiveness, make the request and say, "Help me release this. Guide me and show me." Because on some level, you're not angry at yourself, you're angry at –

let's just give it a name – God, energy. You're angry at the All That Is: "How dare you do this to me? I planned my life *this* way." Do you see how ridiculous that is? [Laughs]

Tony:

Oh yeah. You really, really, really dropped a bomb – I mean in a good way. You're right. I've got to let it go.

Marlise:

What are you meant to do in this lifetime, Tony? You've been transmitting anger. How can you help people from that place? How can you help yourself? Ask to be healed of that, and ask to be filled with love instead. And allow that love to move through you. When I had that experience of that incredible Energy, it literally dropped me to my knees. I had already forgiven my father – but in that moment I wept for him. I wept for him because I realized in his entire life he would probably never have an experience of that kind of Love.

If you have one moment of connection to *That* then passing on is not the worst thing that can happen. Every person who's ever had a near-death experience does not complain about it. They're always willing to go back. So that's not the worst news. The worst news is dying without ever connecting to who you really are.

Tony:

Yeah. I agree. I would never have agreed until right now. Wow. I agree. I feel it. I know what you're talking about, and I want it to continue. I think I need to do it all over again – the whole program, because it's working. And my main thing now is my life. And what's happening to me is working out. I'm not looking for miracles – I just want to be where I'm at.

epilogue

The woman Tony wanted to ask forgiveness of was his former fiancée who he walked away from after being diagnosed with this frightening disease – and who is now back in his life. He didn't even have to look for her – she found him. When you consistently connect and request universal intelligence to enliven and inform your life – it does. From bitterness to acceptance, from anger to forgiveness, from shutting out the world, to letting it in – life was changing.

Tony is an impressive example of the human spirit and what exists within each one of us that is courageous, committed, and willing to do whatever is needed to live in that flow of life. Miracles began happening for Tony early in the program, and his commitment to incorporating what he learned, continued to bring more of them. The way I see it, Tony is the biggest miracle of all – not because of the heroic valor of a dying man, but because of the spirit of one who has chosen to live life with an open heart, continually discovering the depth and beauty of the most profound knowledge we can ever know.

THE ULTIMATE BRILLIANCE: INNER & OUTER KNOWLEDGE

Knowledge is an extremely important element in attaining your highest potential, and how you define it, and where to get it, will make an enormous difference to your daily life and how you evolve. The *Merriam-Webster Dictionary* defines knowledge as information, understanding or skill that you get from experience or education, also: the state of being aware of something.

Our educational system is mainly knowledge based, with no inclusion of the experiential element from higher learning that develops coherency. In a recent interview, Dr. William Tiller shared his thoughts: "A properly balanced society would divide the time between experiential development of the Self and the infusion of knowledge.

"Ultimately we'll get to the place where mythos and logos will unite. Mythos is looking inward for knowledge. Logos is looking outwards for knowledge. Mythos is thought of as the mystical path. But, in fact, it's the inner path. The logos path is the path of science."[1]

If acquiring knowledge is simply gathering information that doesn't fuel a life of value and greater meaning, what is its ultimate purpose? If knowledge doesn't give you a love of life's adventures and the passion and enthusiasm to enjoy them, or give you the ability to deeply care about yourself and others, what is the point!?

the convergence of knowledge and experience

Scientific advances can make an extraordinary difference to the quality of life and your ability to live from your highest potential if you use it to inform any limiting beliefs you might have, and to embrace more expansive thinking. This is where the two worlds, inner and outer – inner experiential wisdom and outer knowledge – converge. When you are connected to that timeless field of information, it offers you experiences that completely shift your understanding of 'knowledge' and where to attain what truly transforms your entire life trajectory.

What I evidenced in my life, and in the lives of others over the last decade, revealed how radically behavior patterns can change through an experiential connection to that energetic field of information. There are subconscious tapes in your brain, recording and replaying the traumatic events in your life, or that of a parent or grandparent, that are unconsciously imprinting your future right now. Thoughts like *you're not good enough* or *what you want is impossible* have set deep grooves that are on constant replay.

Developing experiential evidence for yourself supports new beliefs that become conscious habits. This is why I developed the various SOS Tools you will learn in this section to find more ways of integrating higher consciousness into everyday. Each tool includes the potential of that higher wisdom activated by the Stillness Session Technology, and assists you in putting a directed focus on a specific area. In this way, you draw knowledge from the inner world as well as the outer: mythos and logos.

evolutionary, mind-bending understanding

As I began to contemplate this New Science and the knowledge it is bringing us, alongside what I witnessed in case studies over the years – the phenomenal events that happened to people as they connected with that advanced life Energy stream – new questions emerged. Beyond the research of people meditating and what happens in their brains in a physiological manner,[2] what hasn't been studied is the effects subtle energies have in people's lives; how detrimental patterns and often addictions can be radically altered in much less time than we have thought possible. Having evidence of this helps us all to leave more outdated beliefs behind that have stopped us from recognizing our true potential.

What do you imagine is happening in the cellular structure of the entire body that could cause this level of change? How does that affect your negative tendencies, your health, and why you make the choices you do? What is happening in the brain? Why do you then suddenly stop repeating so many of the patterns that made you unhappy? This is important to reflect on as it gives you insight into what an extraordinary future looks like for you and for us all.

mythos, inner knowledge: infinite potential

You want to activate your brain's abilities to *support you*. It's important to remember that *you* are not your brain – you are more closely related to the ever-expansive *knowing* that ancient teachings speak of, that exists in the depths of Stillness. The Awareness of this unified field is not even defined by the *Merriam-Webster Dictionary*. Some call it

. universal intelligence, Source, or All That Is; whatever name you choose, it is that *super-awareness* that informs your mind and body to release destructive patterns, and replace them with aliveness, contentment, hopefulness and deep peace.

Your ability to consistently connect with this limitless knowledge is integral to attaining your highest potential and living a life you love. The Making Requests Tool was designed to instill a wave of information that calms your mind and offers you a greater sense of security, and knowing that whenever you have a pressing question or concern the answer of what to do will always be there. Making Requests deepens your understanding of your capabilities. You begin to trust more as evidence appears that demonstrates the many benefits this form of obtaining knowledge brings.

we are hardwired for flexibility

We are *designed to evolve*; understanding this you can embrace change with flexibility. Like a butterfly emerging from a cocoon, what you experience is expansive, natural and empowering. Adding the experiential factor of Stillness Sessions to your focus in Making Requests, heightens your ability to access the most profound and yet practical knowledge available that truly makes a difference in your life.

FROM ANGER & EXPECTATION TO ACCEPTANCE & FORGIVENESS

Michael was angry, smoked pot daily, and was smart enough to realize he was stuck in a cycle of pain. The fact that he was adopted, estranged from his kids, and not happy clarified for him that something was amiss, but he wasn't sure what to do about it. One day he reached out on Facebook, hoping to find some answers. As is the way with universal intelligence, the perfect orchestration soon arrived. Something on the website called out to him, entreating a moment of repose. Michael began a course of study with The Simplicity of Stillness that gave him the knowledge he was looking for – that there was a way out.

SOS became an integral practice and as the years passed, many of Michael's detrimental habits began to diminish. The emotional rage that used to devastate those around him didn't appear as frequently, he no longer smoked pot at every meal, and the dramatic roller coaster of life seemed not quite as tumultuous as it had been. And, as it happens, when you have invited in answers from the field of all knowing – they appear. Sometimes they can be events that will demonstrate to you that life has indeed changed. One way this can happen might even be when 'triggered' memories from the past appear. Michael described what one of these events looked like in a note he shared with me:

"My brother and I went together to visit our mom, who is in a retirement home. She is 90 now. She wanted to hold his hand, and I also offered her mine. She held on to the two of us and settled down from the agitated state she had been in.

"Then my brother had to leave on an errand. She immediately pushed my hand away and with a scowl on her face said, 'You can go.' She then closed her eyes and ignored me. I ran away from home at 14 because of this woman. What she did yesterday really hurt me. I did a Stillness Session when I got home. When I woke up this morning I still felt sad and hurt. Then I listened to 'This is Love' (Stillness Session).

"I realized that I should thank her, as my first impulse on returning home yesterday was to get some weed and roll a joint. Get stoned, escape this pain. I did not.

"I saw that my years of drug taking were a result of my hurt. Also as a result of the expectation I had of how a mother should behave. She never lived up to my expectation of what a mother should be like. So for years I carried my resentment around and it would bubble up in me just below the surface.

"I destroyed many a loving relationship, hurt myself, and others, all because I was angry at her and my birth mother. It was a surprise to realize that she still had the ability to cause me pain. I was surprised that I still held the expectation of a loving mother. I still put that on her. My mistake.

"Yet I was happy this morning when I realized, I did not run to drugs, I had not sought refuge in escape. I sat with the pain I had ultimately created for myself, through my expectation of her.

"Then I sent her love and light and wished her well. She is behaving from her understanding (and past) and who am I to judge her path to the light. May she find her love within."

INSIGHTS, QUESTIONS & REFLECTIONS

Can patterns that are unconscious change? Is it possible to respond differently in situations that trigger old memories? While we all know how difficult it can be to change deeply engrained habits – it is possible. Infinite intelligence breaks the rules. *Awareness + new 'mental environment' (new ways of thinking) = transformation.* Michael had been studying higher learning for years, and SOS applied as a consistent practice began shifting his awareness and dissolving the cellular memory that caused him to react in the way he did. Now he had a choice – not to *react* to painful situations, but to find a new course of action, because he could see what had been hidden from view. When cellular memory blocks your inherent knowing, there are fewer choices.

Many people realize that you don't have to react to unpleasant situations that have caused you to feel resentment and anger, but that doesn't help them when triggers create chemical imbalance in the body. What caused Michael to respond differently? The conscious awareness that caused a shift in his perception created an entirely different emotional response. Once his brain was rewired to look for better answers, it was easier for him to respond in a new way – by taking the time to practice the method, he was able to stop, reflect, *act on the inspiration that arrived*, and make better choices.

Can forgiveness rewire your brain to experience more compassion in your life? Or does having compassion rewire your brain to be able to forgive? Accessing infinite Love inspired Michael to *choose* forgiveness. The research of monks (*see Part 3*) who meditated on compassion for many hours revealed *more* gamma waves, indicating that consistent practice could have assisted their remembrance of compassion more rapidly than the other participants.

Could the amount of 'generational pain' you carry have anything to do with your ability to change self-defeating patterns? What is clear is that transgenerational bonds can be broken, regardless of how much or how little you have. (*see Epigenetics, Part 3*). The difference in the length of time for each person might have to do with his or her level of engagement with the processes that eliminate cellular memory, and develop higher consciousness.

REFLECTION: **Do you believe you have limiting patterns that can't change? Are you willing to take steps to dissolve this belief?** Making Requests guides you to the next step. Remember, nothing is permanent.

FROM HARDWIRED THINKING TO REWIRED CAPABILITIES

It was that special time that appears in youth, when you want to see it all, do it all, and be open to the total adventure of what life has to offer you. Maybe it was this venturesome spirit that got two teens from Oklahoma's bible belt to attend a Simplicity of Stillness Program, as it was slightly out of the realm of their daily life choices.

It was definitely an eye-opener, and later that evening I overheard them talking in depth about God, religion, the world, spirituality, and the many views of their friends and relatives. Knowledge is key to evolving in life and it appeared that the lens of the camera had opened wide for these young women.

About a month later, an urgent message was left on my voice mail, "I really need to talk to you. Please call."

The air was thick with unease; Ashley spoke the truth that had been concealed for so long. "I have a problem … and I've been hiding it. I didn't even think it was a problem, but now I know it is, and I just can't live with it any more. I think about food all the time and when I get upset or worried I eat everything in sight – like two pizzas, a quart of ice cream and a box of cookies all at once.

"It's important to look good. It's important to be thin. It's important not to have any problems. That's how it is here. I can't really talk to anyone about it. I don't study, I don't enjoy being with people, nothing is working, nothing. I just can't keep living like this."

Anger, sadness, confusion and then tears – Ashley circled through a round of emotions and then circled through them again. I knew how she felt. After all, like Ashley, I had grown up with an alcoholic – and you can't live around that level of dysfunction and not have it show up somewhere in your life. Only most people stuff it down – *if I don't see it, it doesn't exist.* And for a while the pain is sufficiently hidden, where you don't have to deal with it. Only the pain doesn't really leave – it shows up later in the form of some illness or disease.

Ashley wanted me to 'fix' her problems, and I would have done anything to help her. My heart ached, but I knew that if I solved her problems, it wouldn't help her in the long run. She needed to discover the power she already had. I reminded her that Making Requests was one of the SOS Tools that had given her solutions she loved, and it could bring her that guidance again.

Her tone shifted to that incredulous rancor that teens specialize in, "What!? Really??" I could almost hear her thoughts through the phone lines. *Wasn't I going to help her?! Tell her what to do? How to get school not to fail her if she left before finals? How to find a rehab center that she could get in – right now!?*

If Ashley chose to practice what lights up those circuits of our innate brilliance, I knew it would give her insight that could solve her immediate difficulties. It would also remind her of the potential she had which would be equally important for her biggest hurdle, that of rehabilitation. What Ashley was about to discover is that you can participate in creating the *reality* that surrounds you – and how focusing on what is meaningful to you impacts that reality. She just had to apply the tools, and the answers would come.

Less than a week later, Ashley's rapid-fire excitement shot across the phone lines: "I don't have to fail school! I found a center to go to! And … I'm leaving tomorrow!

"I kept remembering how you've shown me that nothing is impossible, so when all my teachers turned me down and told me they would fail me if I left, I had this idea to email the Dean (of the University) – that maybe somehow he could help. It usually takes a looooong time to get an appointment, but he emailed right back and I met with him the next day.

"He said no one should have to suffer like that, and then he set up appointments to meet all of my teachers with me. Amazing things happened! One of my teachers even began to cry. She told us this really sad story that happened in her own life where she wished she had spoken up, and didn't. Then she told me she was proud of me for having the courage to speak about something that was so uncool. By the end of the day, all my teachers agreed I could leave and take my tests when I return!"

Ashley's journey to heal the unconscious wounds that appeared was already touching other people's lives. Just how many more would be affected by her authenticity and fearlessness, we can only imagine. It was already cracking open the hearts of everyone who watched as the courage she had gained gave her the strength to move mountains. The impossible became a reality as Ashley took the steps needed toward claiming a new life.

When Ashley came out of rehabilitation she was glowing, happy, feeling more secure about herself and her body. She shared with me many of the insights she had gained, about herself, and how seeing the challenges other young women faced helped her to look more deeply at her own.

Taking just a bit of time to focus on Making Requests galvanized events she couldn't have even imagined. Even in the most difficult times, there is guidance, there are answers. Retrieving them is up to you.

INSIGHTS, QUESTIONS & REFLECTIONS

How was Ashley able to access inspiration when she appeared to be in the midst of such an emotional situation? She remembered how well Making Requests actually works, which gave her hope, and she regained the calm needed by listening to a Stillness Session. Even though she was very stressed at the time of the call, she didn't continue the bulimic behavior, and was able to focus on Making Requests to receive guidance. Insight arrived that inspired her next steps (to call the Dean) – *and* the sea of potential that she connected with by applying the process, drew the extraordinary circumstances that occurred into her life.

Did the bulimia return? She has not had the illness in over eight years. What could have caused this healing? Many people have healed in a similar manner (*see Prelude and Step Over That Line*) – when that Energy potential she connected with in the program cleared blockage in her body, her awareness skyrocketed, and she was now ready to take steps to alleviate this harmful pattern. And, although we each have layers to release, not all blocks are eliminated right away.

Did all her addictive tendencies disappear? What research has shown me, is that when we don't internally heal the cause of the addiction, it eventually returns in another area. After healing from bulimia, Ashley stopped doing all inward practices. Several years later, she got involved with a crowd who drank excessively and she joined them. As I reflected on her situation, it reminded me of my own journey to heal the past. While my addictions with drugs and alcohol were resolved rapidly from my connection with this healing potential, other addictive patterns took more time.

As seen in *Wordless Insights*, and other stories, it's clear that emotional pain can be healed. But each person has their own unique journey. Ashley comes from a line of alcoholics, on both sides of her family. Epigenetics (*see Part 3*) helps to explain some of the challenges she is facing. Some people will find a way to heal in this lifetime, others won't. Both Ashley's father and mine died from illnesses related to alcoholism. The more you connect to the inner power, the more healing occurs. While Ashley recently stopped drinking, my concern is that without including powerful inward practices in your recovery, it could be easy to start up again.

Do detrimental tendencies show up at different times in our lives to assist in finding greater strength within because it's needed for advancement in our spiritual journey? Illness, addictions and challenges of all kinds are often the impetus for people to look deeper and want to change. It teaches you to have compassion for those who are struggling. I don't think our challenges have to be a driving force, but they often are – and, what you learn is worth every ounce of what it takes to experience that Love within.

REFLECTION: Sending love and compassion, is one way to support others to find their way home. As we recognize our own frailties, we are inspired to create new roadmaps for others. Try it and see what answers come to you.

MAKING REQUESTS
why, when & how

Making Requests is an invitation to receive greater knowledge, a way to communicate with the creative principle, your personal guidance system. Making Requests generates the emergence of uncommon results. Similar to the inherent properties of a magnet, it attracts answers from that field of universal intelligence that illumines and empowers your choices and decisions. The more you focus that beam of attention in the direction of what you want to know, you'll draw answers, solutions and inspiration that ease and exhilarate your mind.

Why is Making Requests important to me?
There are ingenious, innovative and infinitely intelligent answers to what concerns you, and to guide your every action. Obtaining this knowledge profoundly influences your entire life. Overwhelm, worry and anxiety dissipate when you have answers to what you believe is an impossible or difficult situation.

The more evidence you have of how simply you're able to access answers, the more you trust in the inherent knowing that is *always* there. Day-to-day living becomes an adventure; flexibility, playfulness and inner satisfaction become the new norm.

When do I apply Making Requests?

Making Requests can become a conscious habit to receive inspired guidance on life's most difficult decisions *as well as* the simple ones you make each day. It can be woven into your life to develop clarity, overcome challenges, or just to gain insight on new avenues of enjoyment. What you are shown is the next step of what to do; it is not meant to be an ultimate destination answer. There is comfort and security in knowing that guidance is always there.

SOS TOOL:
MAKING REQUESTS

1 APPLY TOOL & TEACHING:
  a. **Explore**/review SOS Teaching
  b. **Reflect with Three Breath Awareness**
  c. **Write** one Request – suggested formats:
    • **Allow** what is needed to become clear …
    • **Guide** me to the best way …
    • **Assist** a greater understanding to appear …

2 ACTIVATE ENERGY POTENTIAL THROUGH
STILLNESS SESSIONS TECHNOLOGY:
  a. **Listen** to a **Deep State Stillness** or **Sacred Word**. Invite the
     source of creative potential to ignite answers.

3 ACT ON INSPIRATION AS IT IS REVEALED:
  a. Listen for messages and insights – some could appear now
     and also in the days and weeks ahead.
  b. Follow through. Realize it is just the next step, and that
     there will be more to come.
  c. Journal what happens – this way you'll have evidence that
     answers always arise to guide you, which encourages you to
     make this tool a part of your life.

SPECIAL TIP: Requests are not made with the expectation that whatever is asked, should manifest. Instead, they are made with an attitude of appreciation, as one would approach a mentor, a book of great knowledge, or a sacred experience that can offer higher learning and wisdom.

Requests are invitations to reveal the next step, which includes the possibility that the answer could be one you have not even thought of. Once the Request has been made, it's time to listen for the answers in everything that surrounds you. Some answers appear right away, while others are meant to become visible through the journey of discovery laid out before you. Keep it simple, and you will soon find it becoming a habit you love.

EXPANDING INTUITIVE ABILITIES
conscious living: embracing your innate potential

Living connected to your intuitive nature dramatically elevates communication, collaboration and perception of your true potential. It enhances your ability to navigate hazards before they begin and find solutions for those in existence.

Exceptional abilities that have been dormant are unleashed as a consequence of your focus on Expanding Intuitive Abilities. Uncommon characteristics appear as a consequence of your attunement with the intelligent Energy stream of life.

As your senses alight, you learn how to listen to an expansive knowing where you become filled with enthusiasm, and a passion for sharing this infinitely freeing wisdom with others through your natural talents. By embracing your innate power, you are redefining what conscious living is in the world today.

STEP OVER THAT LINE
the wondrous knowing in you

The hellfire in his voice resounded through the church as he dared anyone at the revival to step over that line, the one he made just below the pulpit. *If you don't trust in God, if you don't believe in his almighty power to send you to hell, then step over that line and let it be known.* Everyone hurriedly left the church. Everyone, that is, except the eight-year-old grandchild of this formidable man, the god-fearing minister of the Smoky Mountain congregation.

"Why would God want to send us to hell?" This question had been playing in Robyn's mind for quite some time. She hadn't told anyone, as thoughts like these could get you in trouble. But today was the day she had to find out for herself. As boldly as her granddaddy had challenged his fellowship, the tiny blond-haired child stepped over the line, looked up into the heavens and stated her own demands, " What are you going to do about it?!"

By the time Robyn walked out of the church, she had gotten her answer. She knew God was love – and, she knew there was more that she wanted to know. From Baptist to Catholic, to Buddhism, to chanting, and reading about Gandhi, her thirst was insatiable. This unrelenting search unknowingly became the perfect backdrop to guide her through the rough roads ahead.

the pain, the panic, the day-to-day reality

Life wasn't always easy growing up. Sure, she had the love of her parents, friends and neighbors, but her dad worked a lot, was gone a lot, her mom was stressed, and there wasn't a lot of money to spare. When she found that taking care of people was something she loved to do, and was offered a job straight out of high school to work at a local nursing home, she jumped at it. After all, she already had a lot of practice from taking care of the ailing minister in his final days and her grandmother who was close behind.

Robyn never complained, but her body cried out what she couldn't voice from the stress of the long nights and the difficulties most caregiving represents. She began having panic attacks, and then tunnel vision. Her body sent messages of shooting pain from head to toe. If anyone simply touched her back or her legs, she would cry out in agony. Robyn's 20s turned out to be quite painful, not anywhere near the fun she had imagined.

By the time she was 35, she couldn't take it any longer, depression and medicated drugs had taken their toll. Her tiny frame that had averaged 135lb was suddenly in the 240 range and going up. A bypass helped and the weight came down, but it didn't alleviate the constant pain. Her doctors told her she had fibromyalgia and arthritis in her hands and feet. This wasn't the news she wanted to hear, but it wasn't as bad as the call that brought everything in her life to a grinding halt: "Your mother's in the hospital, she has less than a month to live."

The family was in shock. How could this happen so suddenly? Patsy had acute respiratory distress syndrome, was on a ventilator, and had been placed in an induced coma. After a month, when the doctors wanted to shut it down, Robyn knew that it didn't have to end that way. With a defiance reminiscent of the blond-haired little girl, she looked directly at the doctors, and spoke what was in her heart: "You don't know my God!! And, you don't know my momma!! She is coming home!"

uncovering the unconscious and the super-conscious

Everything she had studied over those years now surfaced to assist her. She listened to the knowing within and each day she sat by her mother's side, sending love. Robyn found that she was guided to do specific healing work; intuitive abilities appeared, revealing insight of what to do. Within just days, her mother was moved to recovery! Shortly thereafter, the doctors reported that her mother could go home, and not only that – there was absolutely "no scarring on her lungs!"

Mom was coming home! It was a joyous event for the entire family. But it also had a downside – one that Robyn wasn't comfortable sharing with anyone. *Where did these gifts come from? How could she have healing abilities like this? Maybe God would be angry.* She was deeply concerned, but held her secret close, just as she had her questions to God those many years ago. But the trauma of the last years, the many challenges she had faced, with taking care of so many people, and not doing such a good job with her own health was about to come to a head.

when pain becomes the messenger

Robyn's Dad was diagnosed with ALS, amyotrophic lateral sclerosis, another illness with a death warrant attached to it, where few live beyond 3–5 years after diagnosis. When she arrived at the ALS Center with her father, she was hit by a severe panic attack; shaking from head to toe, she began to sob. "I can't take it. It's just too much stress on my body." Robyn felt she had to be calm – after all, they were counting on her to be the strong one. The coming weeks proved to only escalate her anguish. "My hands would hurt so bad that I couldn't move them. My feet would hurt, my legs would hurt, I would be so miserable because this pain inside my body was just excruciating. I'd wake up every morning in tears."

Robyn's inner cry was to know more; how to be of service to the people she so dearly loved, how to better understand her own unique abilities, and discover what could be causing all this pain within herself. An invitation appeared to join a scientific study that would focus on people with ALS, and their caregivers. Maybe, just maybe, she would find some answers there.

learning, listening, discovering

During the eight-week SOS Program, Robyn's commitment to her family and her own journey fueled all that she was meant to learn. At one point, her father's raging anger became so intense, she almost packed up and went home, "He wouldn't listen, he just wouldn't hear what I had to say!

"It got so bad that I wanted to leave. I wanted to say, 'I have had enough and I'm going home because I shouldn't be treated this way!' And then I'm thinking, 'What more can I possibly do that I haven't done?' And so I did my *Stillness Session* and *Making a Request*, 'What can I do?' 'What can I do?'' The answers came. Robyn learned to not take on her father's pain, after getting the insight that he needed to express it and physically release his anger. "He got upset today a little bit because he couldn't move very well. So he started screaming, and thrashing about, and fighting, and stomping his feet. And I said, 'Daddy, that's so good. Keep doing it. Let out that anger! Let me see how mad you are. That's wonderful.' He looked at me like I was crazy.

"He's feeling it, acting on it, and I'm allowing it, instead of shutting it down, not wanting him to be angry or upset. I was telling him not to do it before, 'Don't be angry, Dad,' but now I'm allowing it. And he's better for it. I've become so much more calm in dealing with him."

Week after week, new insight surfaced. What once caused Robyn to react in anger or upset, she now handled with ease. Even though the challenges didn't all disappear, she was able to deal with them in an entirely new manner.

One day we were speaking, and suddenly the big secret that had been festering like a wound that never heals was spoken into the light of day. Robyn shared the phenomenal events of her mother's retreat from death's door, and the fears that had grown from facilitating her return to health. *What if only God was meant to heal, and maybe what she was doing wasn't right? What if it was a sin?*

I spoke to her in a language she knew well, the teachings of her youth. Could we become God's hands? Could we be instruments for universal intelligence by *tuning in*, by listening to the messages, and being of service? Gifts from God, intuitive or otherwise, are meant to be shared, to be offered in service. They are not ours to hold on to, but to give back to the world with love.

I could almost hear her sigh of relief. She could finally accept herself, just as she was. In the following weeks, Robyn spoke on one of the calls with the caregivers about the many changes that had begun to appear in her life, "I don't know where I'm at ... I keep climbing up and I just keep reaching up. And it's little by little. And, it's so much better each time I take another step. I just feel myself lightening the load even more with every single step. And I just feel that happiness ...

"And it doesn't matter if I'm stuck in the house all day or I'm stuck here for two weeks at a time, because I haven't been out in like two weeks – and I'm still happy. It's just within me.

"I keep feeling this warmth come over my body, into my hands, into my feet, and it goes out through my head. It's the most amazing, powerful feeling I believe I've ever felt in my life because it's so cleansing. And it just keeps getting better."

The healing power within the program continued its work, dissolving the beliefs that caused her suffering, opening portals that would soon define inherent gifts that were hers to claim. In the final weeks what Robyn received was another present, one she didn't expect that brought her even more joy, despite the wintry weather that kept her locked inside.

the unexpected and exquisite flow of life

"It was really rough there for a time, but the Stillness Sessions and the Divine Love, Divine Will (Sacred Word recording) that, to me, is so peaceful, it brings me a level of being calm. And I didn't realize for the last two weeks that I have been feeling *no pain in my body*, which is a miracle in itself, because I have really bad fibromyalgia – *and I don't anymore*! In the last two weeks it's just gone! I've had it for so many years ... and it's gone!"

As Robyn attuned to the higher influences, many areas of her life began changing, acceptance of herself soothed her soul, and her intuitive gifts expanded. The excruciating pain of whatever beliefs affected or induced her illnesses had dissipated into the unconsciousness from where they arose. She began living from that knowing within. Soon, people were being drawn to her where she could begin to realize these intuitive abilities and use them in service of others. She assisted a man with bipolar disorder to not commit suicide, and a woman with PTSD to become calm in a tense situation. They were guided to the light shining through Robyn; and simply by talking to her some could feel the vital Energy resonating from her, healing their internal pain, giving them a sense of complete calm.

How can this be? When we attune to that exquisite flow of life and live in accordance with it, our true potential arises in many forms. Robyn was ready to discover the continuum of her evolutionary gifts. She was always an extraordinary person, but unconscious beliefs were wreaking havoc in her life. Conscious living is about seeing what you couldn't before, and aligning with the abilities that are your birthright. If you walk the journey with an open heart and mind, with curiosity and commitment, as Robyn did, your life will reflect that same loving, and impassioned Energy resonating through you.

epilogue

During her father's final days and after he passed away, Robyn found that the calm she had accessed in the program had now become a part of her. She wasn't affected by stress in the way she was before, as she now managed life's challenges differently.

While Robyn hadn't told people about the escalation of her intuitive and healing abilities, people were suddenly being drawn into her life; she knows this is happening so she can learn more about how to offer these gifts to others. Robyn also noticed that the form of her healing abilities had changed and was excited to continue deepening her study.

The fibromyalgia hasn't returned, and I don't imagine it will; as of this writing, it's been 11 months since the pain and symptoms dissappeared. Robyn's future is filled with so much that is unknown, and yet she feels intuitively that she is on the perfect journey. She has even begun speaking to her mother about selling their property and moving on. Whatever happens, one thing is for sure, that *knowing* within will be there, guiding her to whatever adventure she is ready to take.

YOUR INTUITIVE INTELLIGENCE
listening to the messages

You have an exceptional intelligence waiting to be utilized *beyond* your usual thought patterns. These intuitive abilities become evident as psychological and physiological limitations formed over time are eliminated.[1] When these beliefs and blocks dissipate, your cognitive and perceptive senses ignite. It's like entering an information highway with search engine optimization programmed to find wisdom and enlightened guidance at every stop. You are directed from a higher understanding that merges hope with multilevel gifts; rather than downloading senseless thoughts that result in upset and overload, you *hear*, *see*, *feel*, and *intuit* messages that are purposeful and value driven.

multidimensional intuitive awareness
What does being attuned to sensory perception, progressively advancing higher consciousness look like? You are powerful *and* thoughtful, compassionate *and* assertive, courageous *and* peaceful. You are able to identify old patterns rapidly, release them, and use the messages you receive to shift back into the conscious flow that has become a way of living. You listen to other points of view, while looking for synergistic solutions – and initiate cooperation that inspires and stimulates innovation.

a reality that engenders new beliefs

As remarkable points of reference multiply in the library of your life, they change your beliefs. This expands the field of your potential where true harmony and coherence originates. Assimilating higher intuitive perception doesn't mean you will never have another doubt or time when you appear to trip – that's just another part of the chipping away process to get to the gold. It's a signpost that arrives to guide you to traverse whatever divide has arisen with the knowledge that greater benefits can only become visible when you go beyond where you are and what you know. When concepts leave you, the strengths you gain invite deeper introspection.

What are you meant to realize at this point in your evolution? What intuitive talents do you want to expand? Through these processes The Simplicity of Stillness ignites, greater insight and clarity arise as blocks of all kinds are released. A higher intelligence becomes apparent in various ways. Your mind becomes more agile, a dynamic flow of information reveals that you are never shut off from this remarkable current of knowledge. What you discover is that your abilities accelerate through direct focus on the area you wish to excel. Upgrading these innate skills offers wisdom into a new reality.

your brilliant intuitive senses: clairvoyance, clairsentience, clairaudience, and claircognizance

Expanding your intuitive abilities opens life choices as you now have a reach beyond what you thought possible. Depending on your ability to allow universal intelligence to speak to you, and flow through you, will define how rapidly your senses become attuned. They expand exponentially through consistent connection, focus and intent (*see Step Over That Line, Simply, Powerfully Beautiful*).We all have exceptional skills, only we haven't known how to unleash them and tune in. The talents and gifts that accelerate in the coming months are not meant for an ego to suddenly believe it has attained something that others don't have – but rather to use the insight to increase your capacity for communication, collaboration and the sheer joy of living.

In a report on the *60 Minutes* television program, a small group of people demonstrated that our brains are capable of more than we have ever considered. These people have the capacity to recall *everything* that has happened on any given day in their lives, and in history, *within seconds of asking them*. Everything! From what they had for breakfast to what the headlines were in the newspaper. They are not savants; they just have an ability that very few of us have. If this is possible, then what else haven't we yet considered?

Each of us is equipped with the perfect set of abilities to live our life's purpose. Imagine accessing that part of the brain that is untapped. Imagine allowing the dynamic subtleties of higher energies to wipe the slate clean of anything that might have darkened your brilliance. This is about merging human intelligence with universal intelligence. It's not about learning tricks, and many of you will discover abilities surfacing that are truly phenomenal.

Meditation masters have long warned people of *siddhis*, the gifts that arrive along your journey to know the highest – and not to get swayed by them. These abilities are not the goal; they are qualities of your potential to be put in service of the whole of humanity.

our lives are changing

It's important to grasp the enormity that the tool, Expanding Intuitive Abilities represents, so that you can believe, invite and allow in your innate inheritance. Notice how it happened for each of the people in this chapter, how it benefitted every part of their lives. Your Energized focus and what you receive increases through your participation. Untapped gifts will appear to bring higher consciousness and mastery into your life. As they multiply you will find this creative impulse transmitting joy, enthusiasm and confidence into each day.

This evolutionary, ever-evolving highway that we are on can be all that you envision. Staying open and flexible is part of the journey. Imagine what can happen for you, and let it inspire you to take the next step – don't wait til the final bell rings to embrace it. You get to define the road ahead. Be sure to take the time to continually explore what these gifts can teach you about creating a magnificent world and life you love.

FLIGHTS OF HOPE AND PROMISE

He grew up on the plains of Africa, a Maasai, the renowned warriors of Kenya, many who live their lives today much as their forefathers have for centuries. He learned the ways of the land, carried a spear as a child, and was raised with the same cultural education as those of his tribe.

The providential crossroads where lives were meant to intersect were miles from anywhere, in the middle of the vast African continent. After the rains washed away the already unsuitable roads that were to take me back to my lodge, an invitation from my guide to stay at his home was truly impossible to turn down. Quite unexpectedly, plans were set to stay in a Maasai village, in what would be a fortuitous night, setting in motion a sense of the sublime and memorable events to come.

destiny arrives seemingly out of nowhere

When the clouds parted, an opportunity arose to build a campfire, and before long there were countless warriors circling the blazing light. My guide suddenly stood, and announced that I could show them a way to find a *power* within – *and that now was the perfect time*! The illuminated Energy carried on the waves of the music intensified as the Stillness Session played, one man experienced a profound shift breaking through the depression he had. Amidst the remarkable events that appeared for these sons of Kenya in the coming days, it clarified for him in that moment, that his life was about to change.

Action Jackson's eyes sparkled with the newfound happiness he felt as he invited me to return the next day and teach this magical method to the women and children at the clinic where he worked. When I arrived, Jackson spoke to me of a vision he had that carried him through the demanding situations he faced, where day after day he attended the sick and destitute people at the clinic. His dream was two-fold – to become a Maasai balloon pilot so he could make more money to run the clinic, and to shift the understanding of his people with regard to the long-standing cultural practice of circumcision.

Jackson spoke of his depression in the previous months, when all that ran through his mind was, *"It's impossible. It will be so much money."* There were arduous and economic challenges at every turn, and he had begun to lose the optimism that higher aspirations evoke. *Maybe his dreams were only lofty ideals*, as many now joked. Jackson felt the pangs of hopelessness for the first time. But after last night's immersion into the heart-palpitating experience[1] of his innate power, he had a *knowing* that his dream was meant to happen. He didn't know *how*, but a renewed conviction had surfaced, a *deep sense* that was stronger than his doubts, telling him that yes, it would happen.

This Maasai lived without borders in his mind; he lived a life of service – a visual essay of honesty, compassion and goodness. But the road ahead would not be an easy one. I told him I would dedicate the proceeds of my next Stillness Session recording to support his dream and that we would stay in touch.

signposts can be what you least expect

The next year was a time of political unrest in Kenya and the drought added even more tension. Travel slowed, communication was cut off, and no tourists arrived, including friends from overseas who helped with the financial support of the clinic. When the phone lines finally worked, my dear friend spoke about the difficult times people were going through.

I reminded him about the *insight* that had ignited within him, and to listen to those messages, that everything might actually be working out for the best, even when he couldn't see it. Jackson said that he was discovering just how much that deeper knowing was teaching him. He realized there was a reason why nothing seemed to be moving – that he wasn't meant to go to balloon school that year.

Many of the tribes had given him their consent and trust – and more than 137 circumcision ceremonies were performed using the new procedures he taught them! He had even been able to convince some to allow the young men to use local anesthesia to dull the pain. He knew he needed to be there, they trusted him. Beliefs that were locked into the very core of his society – that caused untold pain and even death – were changing because of him. He realized that as much as he wanted to see his dream unfold, maybe being where he was – was exactly where he needed to be.

intuitive abilities, innate gifts

Jackson told me of the unusual events that had begun to happen; the Energy he felt that special night was now transmitting through him, and people could feel it. He spoke of having a deeper cognition that often informed him of what was actually occurring, beyond the outer appearance of the event. And the magical way this intuitive insight would reveal to him whatever was needed to solve the uncommon challenges he faced.

A young man who had been mauled by a lion arrived at the clinic late one night, bleeding profusely. Everyone expected him to die, including his brother, who unbeknownst to Jackson was planning suicide if his brother died. The older brother waited for news through the night, sitting at the foot of the tree outside the clinic door. He felt he was to blame for not being strong enough to save his little brother when the lion attacked.

There were no close hospitals, so Jackson operated on the young man, even though he never had training in this area of medicine. It was a life and death situation. Something came over him, and in that moment he said he *knew* exactly what to do to save him. The boy lived. And so did his brother, who was beaming with joy to find his wide-eyed best friend waiting to greet him in the morning.

At another time, a woman was dying for no apparent reason after giving birth. Jackson couldn't understand it as she was healthy and the birth had gone well. He sensed that she was emotionally in pain, being the second wife of her husband, and that she didn't feel loved. Jackson decided to share his insight with the first wife. On hearing what could be causing the young woman's symptoms, the first wife literally called the woman back from death's door by asking her forgiveness for not loving and including her in the family.

Jackson's new skills had nothing to do with the education needed to medically save lives, and yet, the intuitive capabilities that had arisen in him were doing just that. He had realized so much in the last years as the Stillness became a part of his life. His dreams of becoming a balloon pilot had not left him; his perception had increased, and so had his trust, he *knew* what to do at the perfect time that would benefit everyone. Who knows what might have happened in these people's lives if he hadn't been exactly where he was needed for his and their evolutionary journey to unfold as perfectly as it did.

when a no is a yes in disguise

We continued to correspond; getting a visa to go to flight school was like running into a wall of *no's*. Which in retrospect was perfect, but it was just one more rationale why everyone believed becoming a balloon pilot was *an impossible dream.* Everyone that is, except Jackson, who continued Making Requests, listening to the Stillness Sessions, and inviting the intuitive gifts within to grow.

The hope in Jackson's heart stayed strong. The next year I found a balloon school in California and sent him books to begin the long and arduous study needed to pass the many barriers, mechanical and language, he would soon come up against.

dreams and visions that lead to greater purpose

I had gotten used to living in a state of wonderment by that time, but when I awoke one morning to read an email with flight information of Jackson's arrival, it took my breath away. Jackson had left Africa! *And without even knowing if someone would be at the airport to pick him up!* Jackson had decided it was time for his dream to become real and trusted that it would.

Having a dream, a vision for your future, is not about being irresponsible, it's about being fully responsible for allowing your inner purpose to be realized, so you can love what you do and serve others along the way. There is tremendous power when you take action from that intuitive knowing that arises in the many forms it does. The potential it offers makes the improbable – possible.

I wondered how it would come about, as I wouldn't be able to host him, now that I didn't live in LA full time. But I had also learned to trust that everything would fall into place. I took off to meet him with only enough time to stay for a week and introduce him to a few friends before I had to leave on my next tour.

your life touches others, indelibly and forever

Friends of Jackson became a slogan for the extraordinary group who found themselves aboard his flight of hope. Jackson miraculously passed his first pilot's test, despite the obvious language challenges. The journey wasn't meant to end there. More support would be needed to get him to his ultimate vision – *or* was this also about what was needed to extend hope into even more people's lives?

The inner glow emanating from Jackson lit up everyone who met him; he transmitted such passion and generosity that people were drawn to him wherever he went. In a grocery store, in line to get a cell phone, at picnics and film premieres, people asked to exchange phone numbers. They offered their homes and planned fund-raising events. He spoke at universities, observed surgeries at leading hospitals, taught school children about the Maasai tribe's culture, met with bankers and non-profit directors, gave numerous lectures wherever people would listen about circumcision, malaria and the Maasai – *and* learned how to surf, went fishing, played golf and used a can opener, all for the first time.

His intuitive abilities escalated and were put to use again and again, as the people who were hosting him suddenly found themselves in situations where *they* needed his guidance.

Jackson touched many people's lives, and it brought him a greater understanding of the love and power conscious intuitive living creates. The day after Christmas when Jackson returned to Africa, he took a lot of love and lifelong friendships with him – as well as that glorious certificate, the one that verified dreams do come true. Jackson's commercial pilot's license would soon hang in the clinic in Talek as a testament to the difficulties – withstanding drought, famine, political unrest, and sundry challenges that might have barred most people from ever believing in the impossible – and to the wondrous events that had played out in his and so many people's lives.

Action Jackson's journey offered people a way to recognize the promise of their own dreams – how to create a life of purpose while loving your own. When you live connected to the conscious power within, you can soar through the skies of your imagination as Jackson did long before those flights above the plains of Africa became a reality.

What can't we learn from this ordinary/extraordinary man? He invited the flow of life to teach him, and it did – that it unfolds in the best way possible when you listen, and become attuned to the adventure life truly is. After all, soaring through skies of hope-filled dreams can be anyone's destiny when believing and unleashing those wondrous gifts within.

INSIGHTS, QUESTIONS & REFLECTIONS

Will everyone who does the SOS Method see more intuitive skills appearing in their lives? Most people find that their cognitive abilities skyrocket. And, when you focus directly on them, using the Expanding Intuitive Abilities Tool, it brings into focus exactly what you are aiming at. Keeping a journal is a good idea so you can record the various events as they happen; this way it builds evidence, entraining your brain that you have these skills and that they can expand.

Does everyone have an ability to heal others? Both Jackson and Robyn (*see Step Over That Line*) discovered that the healing Energy field they connected with had begun to be transmitted through them. Each person draws to them the abilities they focus on and that align with their life purpose. Everyone has the ability for self-healing simply by allowing the frequencies of higher consciousness to flow through them. Higher levels of healing abilities can open through consistent connection, practice and intention.

What intuitive abilities do most people find expanding by applying this tool? Claircognizance elevates in most people to a much higher level.It goes from where most people have a gut feeling they don't trust – to a deep knowing – that brings extraordinary benefits when acted on – which usually happens as your level of trust rises, as well as your abilities to discern the difference between the two. Clairaudience and clairsentience seem to open next for many people. Again, it is dependent on where you put your focus and on your level of Energetic connection. This is why Expanding Intuitive Abilities is so helpful as it includes both of these elements.

Does having intuitive abilities assist in all vocations? Yes, as you can see from all three stories in this segment, every person found various capabilities arising that assisted them directly with their vocation and life purpose. Their ability to communicate and collaborate with people extended more love and enjoyment in their lives, and gave them a greater understanding of their personal power.

REFLECTION: **What dream have you let go of? What would you like more insight on? What gifts would you like to see expand?** Applying the SOS Tool at the end of this section will assist you in receiving the inspiration that unleashes and clarifies your abilities by taking them to the next level.

SIMPLY, POWERFULLY BEAUTIFUL

Betsy had what most men and women want – intelligence and looks, she was extremely smart and beautiful. But what she didn't have is what she wanted most – an ability to express herself without always feeling like it was the wrong thing to say, and the wrong time to say it. After the loss of her job as an attorney in a prominent Los Angeles firm, Betsy wanted more than ever to find her true voice.

There'd been men in her life who thought that having a strong point of view was somehow not attractive. So Betsy made decisions somewhere along life's journey that affected her voice and her personality as well. She was so soft spoken you rarely heard her, and was so intimidated she hardly spoke up at all.

Betsy's shortcomings were similar to everyone whose talents are imprisoned in fortresses of their own fears. Various clues to why this happens are appearing through science today (*see Epigenetics*). It lies hidden in the past, and often never surfaces, so people lead lives that don't allow the beauty of their true essence to shine through. Betsy had such difficulty speaking that when she finally gathered her courage, her suggestions would be sprinkled with apologies, "Excuse me but ... I'm sorry ... I'm sorry ... but ..." It was sad to see. You couldn't help but adore her gentle, loving heart, while silently wishing she would find what was holding her back.

and the walls came tumbling down

What transpired next is how the mystical of life appears that often seems out of reach, and yet it is available to even the most skeptical when the time is right. This very classic lady who rarely had a hair out of place, or a wrinkle in her designer suit, had an astonishing vision during her first Stillness Session. When she opened her eyes, there was that look of wonderment, which reveals entry into worlds rarely seen, or insight accessed beyond the normal reach of our senses.

Tears trickled down and joined her whispered words, compelling visions of ages past. Symbols and colors were vividly expressed, a world of imagery became a reality that left an indelible imprint on what the future would present. "There were people sitting all around me. They were dressed in clothes of the different cultures they came from ... and each of them was there to teach me something ... something special ... about me ...".

Particles of Energy can be seen with the naked eye and are palpably experienced when illumined Love is present. Each moment was charged with the timeless presence resonating in the space. When your heart feels that Love it has longed to know for lifetimes, you never want it to end. Betsy was wrapped in the incomparable brilliance of the knowledge she had been seeking in her search to find her voice. It was never about being demanding or forceful in any way, it was simply, "... to know the person I truly am ..."

Her mother appeared in the vision as well, speaking what she couldn't when Betsy was a child. She hadn't taught her to believe in herself, as she hadn't found that recognition within. And, she had never spoken the words all children want to hear, how truly proud she was of her daughter. As Betsy's powers of observation grew, she suddenly realized the depth of her mother's insecurities. This insight, hidden for so long, paved the way for forgiveness, and to release the blame she had carried. Love burst forth in the neglected garden, overgrown with weeds of unconscious discontent. The confirmation of what had held her back accelerated her innate abilities to replace fragility with confidence and fear with stability of character.

one by one, the gifts appeared

The attorney who had been known for her timorous nature had a different countenance when I saw her one week later. She moved with a sense of confidence I hadn't seen before. Betsy said she found comfort listening to the Stillness Sessions and she played them nightly as she drifted off to sleep. A mischievous smile verified that even more had changed, and with a nod of recognition she told me about the uncommon week she had.

When an overbearing man commandeered the conversation at an annual couples' dinner, Betsy responded in a uniquely different manner than she was accustomed to. She stood with determination while still maintaining a thoughtful countenance, and voiced her insight aloud, "Do any of you have something more to add? It would be so nice if we could hear from *all of you*." Silence echoed in the room. Something had shifted, a new energy opened in the space, and soon emboldened conversations were popping up everywhere.

Voices were heard that usually weren't. The evening had a different quality than previous events and was so freeing and enjoyable numerous guests thanked her personally. Betsy's husband looked at her glowing face with the astonishment of one who has seen a race horse win after years of showing in the bottom five, and inquired with wide-eyed confusion, "What has come over you, Betsy? *Who are you?*"

step by step, day by day

Each week as years of pent-up anxiety and feelings of inadequacy left, newfound strength lined the muscles of her stature. Betsy found a love of life surfacing. "I never knew what I wanted before; everything looked so big, so monumental. Now it's easy for me to identify. Nothing's that big; *it's just the next step*." I had to laugh as I wanted to repeat her husband's proclamation, but I couldn't get a word in. Betsy's enthusiasm kept pouring out: "I know I can make things happen. I feel like I am finally the captain of my own ship!"

Talk about a change in perspective! Betsy was being who she always wanted to be: *herself*, a gracious tower of strength. She had this *inner knowing* guiding her now; her ability to perceive a situation in a glance was uncanny. Many new skills appeared, expanding her intuitive abilities, giving her the courage she had never known. No longer a prisoner of constrictive beliefs, she was out in the world that had once defined her, breaking through to a new life, ready to fulfill her dreams.

angels and attorneys

Two months later Betsy landed a job at one of the most prestigious law firms in Los Angeles. Three months after that, they promoted her to managing partner! It was then this vibrant, intelligent blonde got the dream that had been written on her heart for years – to be second chair in a jury trial. On the day she was called to represent her client in court, Betsy was serenely fearless. She had learned to trust the insights that always made an appearance at the perfect moment. This time was no different.

After speaking to the jury, on her client's behalf, he looked at her with total appreciation and disbelief. Inquiring with absolute sincerity, he spoke the words she had become accustomed to hearing, *"Who are you?"* followed by new ones she had never heard before, *"Are you an angel?!"*

We don't often consider *angels* and *attorneys* as two words that are descriptive of each other, but I imagine Betsy could change our opinion on this. That self-expressed voice she always wanted brought these two worlds together, and I doubt they'll ever be separate again – at least, whenever Betsy is around.

INSIGHTS, QUESTIONS, & REFLECTIONS

Do intuitive skills always expand as rapidly as Betsy's did? And does everyone have visions? People connect with their intuitive abilities in any number of ways as this creative Energy potential is activated; from having visions, to hearing messages, from inspirational writing that seems to arise from somewhere beyond you, to feeling sensations that alert you to take action. As you can see from Jackson to Robyn to Betsy in this chapter, and including many others throughout the book, it happens when we are open, and when it's the best time possible for the advancement of our overall consciousness.

What is meant by true self-expression? Often people get confused about what being self-expressed means – and the pendulum can swing from the pain of not feeling heard to unconscious loud, demanding, and often rude communication. When you have guidance from higher intuitive abilities, you are consistently breaking through into new ways of be-ing; speaking, thinking and taking action. None of it comes from a false bravado; it resonates instead from a place of sincerity, clarity, inspiration and strength.

What can I do if people don't like that I have begun to express myself more? You are on an evolving journey into more conscious living. As you continue to step into new ways of be-ing, there is often a push back from those around you who want life to be the way it was when you were unexpressed. This never works, for anyone. Step lightly into your new life, and invite others to see you for who you really are. They will eventually join the game in the way you have set it up, where each person speaks *and* listens, bringing greater value to the relationship – *or,* you will part ways. Allow your expanded intuitive skills to guide each moment. Notice if the pendulum has swung too far, and be sure to include kindness with your new strengths.

Can I be a quiet person and still be self-expressed? If you choose to be expressed in silence, that stillness can absolutely transmit everything you want to say. And if you are hiding, or feel there is something blocking your true expression, then take the steps outlined here that will guide you to be all that you are.

REFLECTION: **Is there anything you would like to express differently that would make a transformative shift in your life?** Are there intuitive senses you would like to expand? When you are ready, go to the tool, Expanding Intuitive Abilities, or Making Requests, and invite the answers to arrive.

EXPANDING
INTUITIVE ABILITIES
why, when, where & how

To live from your fullest potential requires coherence, where you tap into and use higher sensory perception. Now, by consistently connecting with advanced life Energy, a new language is opening. We know that we are only using a small percentage of our intelligence. Science tells us we are unable to see and hear what has been beyond our (vibrational) comprehension, and what our unconscious beliefs have defined.

The current that flows through this intelligent universe speaks to you in a multitude of ways – but if you are not attuned to it, you won't hear the messages. You could miss out on the remarkable qualities that are your true heritage; that ignite the intuitive mind, and open the loving intelligence of the heart.

When we access the *conscious awareness* that releases outdated belief boundaries, our abilities skyrocket. This is not about becoming a psychic or medium, and many of you are already in tune with any number of these and other extraordinary talents – this is about continuous evolution, where you embrace the next level of your potential.

Why is Expanding My Intuitive Abilities important to me? It changes the way you function every day. As you break through the societal concepts that have hindered innate potential, your exploration of your own innate genius will reveal untapped abilities. The more you connect with this current of multidimensional awareness, it facilitates perceptual expansion in every area of your life. We each have capabilities that are unique and as you explore what they are, you'll discover it exceeds the cerebral education you've been taught.

When do I apply Expanding Intuitive Abilities? At anytime, no matter what is going on, you can tap into higher levels of your intuitive knowing, where you sense what people need before they do, affecting solutions before problems arise. Your *inner knowing* intuits the best place to be at the perfect time, thereby releasing common angst and concerns. Your senses alight and offer you valuable creative insight to deal with the most challenging situations. You become more flexible, not needing to control everything, but flowing with unimaginable circumstances that appear through the trust you have gained.

Where do the messages come from? Messages appear in many forms. Your heightened senses communicate through **what you see** (Clairvoyance), **feel** (Clairsentience), **and hear** (Clairaudience), **and deeply sense or know** (Claircognizance). As you observe the synchronicities that show up, you'll enjoy the wonder that life presents. Some messages appear:

• As a deep *inner knowing*.
• When listening to a friend or a child, or someone speaking through media – and unexpectedly, you *know*, it's like your *senses* have been lit from within.

- An illness or injury that suddenly stops you in your tracks, literally forcing you to look deeper.
- Not getting what you thought you wanted. This can be an invitation to realize something is happening beyond what you can see. Higher guidance is inviting you to reflect. A better outcome arrives by shifting where you are headed.
- Articles that catch your eye – an email arrives with information that specifically answers a question you were holding in your mind.
- When Making Requests, or doing any of the SOS Tools, answers appear, many through your intuitive senses.

SOS TOOL: EXPANDING INTUITIVE ABILITIES

1 APPLY TOOL & TEACHING:

a. **Explore**/review SOS Teaching.

b. **Reflect** with Three Breath Awareness.

c. **Request messages** of what you want to know, of what would support you – to be sent through one of the intuitive abilities listed below:

- **Clairvoyance – is intuitive insight or perceptiveness.** It's like looking with your inner eye, with a second sight. You might see images or symbols as though they are on a movie screen.

- **Clairsentience – is a 'feeling'.** You are able to sense **the energetic vibration of another** – sad, doubtful, distrustful, happy or angry. Some people find they are able to tap into someone at a distance as well.

- **Clairaudience – is an inner sense of hearing.** It's the ability to hear sounds beyond the reach of ordinary experience; these could be names, dates, sayings, songs or melodies. It is different from usual mind chatter, and can relay a message to you.

- **Claircognizance – is an *inner knowing*.** Many people think it a gut sense, but it is *much more* than this. It is when you *deeply know* something, even when you don't know why or how. As you become more attuned, this knowing expands through trust, and even more evidence will appear.

2 **ACTIVATE** ENERGY POTENTIAL THROUGH STILLNESS SESSIONS TECHNOLOGY: Choose from whichever recording calls to you.

3 **ACT** ON INSPIRATION AS IT IS REVEALED: Listen to, write in your journal, and take action on the messages given through the senses in the coming days and weeks ahead.

A new sphere of awareness expands through your innate abilities. Soon you notice it's just the way you live.

TRANSMITTING CONSCIOUS COMMUNICATION
dynamic intelligence: thinking, speaking & transmitting

Your thoughts can develop chemical reactions in your body. Your words send these patterns of influence to your brain. And you experience whatever meaning you give to these architects of life – whether it is joyful or stressful. While many people realize that eliminating detrimental patterns will bring greater ease and joy – what we haven't had is a simple and effective process that helps to eliminate emotional triggers and develop habits that are responsive, intuitive and value driven.

It's not easy to stop the thoughts in your mind from running rampant when you feel you've been mistreated or misunderstood. And yet, when there is a dynamic release of painful cellular memory, it causes a shift in the biochemical production in your body where feelings of happiness, enthusiasm and hopefulness can now surface.

By using the Transmitting Conscious Communication Tool you are continually elevating your dynamic inner intelligence. What this grants you is a greater quality of life – self-expression, creativity, health and prosperity – where you dynamically transmit higher consciousness into your life and the world.

FINDING YOUR TRUTH, FROM PAIN TO PASSION

"I hate my father, I hate my family, there's nothing in my life worth living for." Ana's jet-black hair hung down like a curtain shielding her from the world, her eyes barely visible through the dark glasses she wore. The lighting in the room was dim, and yet in comparison to her thoughts it was a brightly lit space.

Like most teens, Ana didn't have many references to give her the assurance that she was loved, that she was infinitely powerful and that she had tremendous potential. After years of coping with angry thoughts steam-rolling through her mind, possibly giving her the severe migraine headaches she endured, Ana had reached her threshold of pain. She stepped outside the boundaries of her beliefs the day she walked in the door of my offices. Ana's employer suggested she meet with me and find out for herself if this new *Stillness Method* could help her to heal.

This young woman's every thought and action resonated the rage she felt with the world, so much so she was generating even more of it – angry friends to agree with her, angry parents to blame, and an angry mind that was voicing pain so loudly, living with it was becoming unbearable. She closed her eyes with trepidation to try out this "*Stillness thing*," even though in her words, she'd "... never been good at anything like that before." Almost immediately her body shifted its rigid stance as the Energetic force field filled the room, carried on the notes of the liquid music played.

Eyes opened wide with wonder, like a child on Christmas morning, Ana hesitantly shared all that transpired: "The first thing I heard … was angry voices, so many angry voices … and they were all coming from *inside* me.

"And then everything turned to white light, this brilliant white light! And I don't know why, but I feel so happy ..." Her face no longer had the lifeless look so often seen on those who are outraged with this world and their place in it. When I reached out to say goodbye, something inside me ignored her original *keep your distance* signals, and my arms wrapped around her like a mother embracing a lost child. Ana held on to me as though I was a life vest that would save her from drowning in the dark seas that she had been churning in for so long.

As we stood in that timeless moment, I felt a tremendous outpouring of love, as though the force resonating through this universe wanted her to know unequivocally how much she was loved, and was using my form to give her the message. This stream of unconditional Love was flowing with such intensity Ana began to cry … and cry … and cry … and then to laugh, and laugh, and laugh.

What is possible as this power ignites is beyond conventional understanding. Lifetimes of suffering begin to shift, not from an *intellectual understanding*, as nothing anyone could ever *say* could advance that degree of transformation. Something out of the ordinary had occurred that would forever alter the life of this troubled soul, who had now lifted out of the sea of darkness that only an hour before shrouded her every move.

It was Valentine's Day and a surprising gift had arrived at my door. Ana was not the same person from one week before. Her hair was styled so you could see her beautiful face. Dark chestnut eyes sparkled as she asked me with sincerity if she would feel the same happiness today that she felt at her last visit – and if it would continue to stay with her, as it had most of the past week.

I told her how different it is for each person; that some feel a euphoric *high* for days and even weeks before it's integrated into an elevated and more balanced vitality. And, that it was also possible to feel sadness or frustration – and *that* would be just as beneficial, because it would ultimately provide a deeper awareness of a pattern or belief that blocked their joy.

The depth of wisdom received from this evolutionary awareness parallels what the world's philosophers, poets and sages write about in ancient teachings – how lifetimes of distress can be released. It also parallels research from The New Science – how our DNA can change the coding in our cells. The subtle energies coupled on the music of the Stillness Session had set in motion what is of foremost significance in the life of every human being – living in harmony with your very essence.

As Ana embarked into that dimension of Stillness where true healing exists, the alchemy transformed her body's chemistry as well as her mind. There was no need to swig high-octane caffeine drinks, or use stimulants of any kind. A new high replaced what had steeped her in constant turmoil;

calm replaced out-of-control. Ana began living in a new reality, communicating in a way that didn't always revolve around anger. She knew that she was in charge of her life. If she didn't like it, there was no one to get upset with. She understood *she* was responsible for turning it around. What is left in this paradigm of living is extraordinary. Love now replaced the weighted anguish this once depressed teen had carried. What she soon discovered was that she rarely had that level of anger anymore.

When Ana returned for her third and final session, she spoke in a somewhat offhand manner to let me know she was not surprised or impressed – but the agonizing migraines that she'd had for years had stopped. She thought she would have them forever and now they were gone. Ana had quit hanging out with angry friends and found new ones that made her laugh and enjoy life more. She repaired her relationship with her parents, applied to culinary school, and built a business in the coming years where she became renowned for her celebrity clientele. Years passed and one day she sent me a note – a kind of history, about how it all began, and the many changes she had gone through:

"I smoked heavily, drank to forget, ate to suppress, slept with an endless string of 'piss your parents off' kinda guys, and I covered myself in tattoos ... Addicted to this pain ... I created illness in my body as a result. This was the wake-up call. When I was 18, Marlise gave me the tools that allow me to sit in Stillness ... to truly discover what life is.

"To think about where my life was six years ago, the anger that vibrated through me, the fear and negativity that I carried, is almost unbearable. I am not a different person today, but an evolved person. So many changes occurred ... the relationships that ended, the battles that went away, the reactions that ceased, the addictions that just didn't feel right anymore. Relationships that were simply choked by anger and negativity became light, and evolved into understanding and compassionate friendships. "People around me reacted to my new energy. Instead of fighting for my opinion, I just speak the truth and let it be what it is ..."

The conditioned responses Ana had for years, blaming everyone for her medical conditions and unhappy life, continued to dissolve through time as new values lined the neural pathways that would bring her greater strength and courage. Speaking the truth resonated so loudly within, that one day Ana realized she could no longer hold on to a story she had set in motion as a teen; feeling powerless and wanting to manipulate others through empathy, she began telling people she had cancer.

When Ana called to let me know that she had misrepresented the truth to me as well, only weeks before my first book came out – where I shared the elements of the story as it was conveyed to me – I was stunned. I had verified the facts with everyone I wrote about. In both a call and email response she stated that everything was correct. Dismay, shock, sadness. I needed to find an answer that would help me understand. I decided to call a friend and mentor, who had worked with people in his programs for more than 50 years, assisting them to live from integrity and love.

Parked in front of the restaurant, going nowhere, we sat in silence as my tears tried to clear the storm clouds that had been swirling since the call. In a southern drawl spoken only by those from the Deep South, he gently questioned, "Have you forgiven her Marlise?"

The tears that had fallen with only a thought for my own concern, now reminded me of what is of greatest importance – the infinite Love that exists at the heart of all. I had forgotten. I knew what had happened was a lesson for me as well as for Ana. It is one I will never forget. How can you blame another when you don't know what internal suffering they might be going through that you can't see? The recent pain or past influence that might have robbed her of better choices. As I reflected, my astute friend offered me another perspective to consider.

"Marlise, I want you to think about this. What she did, by telling you the truth *now* – really speaks to the power of this method.

"She could have kept this hidden, no one would have known. She risked losing the love of two people who were very important to her – you, and the woman who sent her to you. But she had changed so much from that person who told that story that regardless of the consequences she had to own up to what she had done. She had to speak the truth."

The clarity of his words touched my heart, and I set an Intention, that one day I would be given the opportunity to write *this* story – to set the record straight, and to include the

221

lesson I had learned as well. I called Ana, and amidst a round of tears and even laughter, our hearts melted into one. And, isn't that where true healing begins, through the pulsation of Love, as you *speak the truth and let it be ... exactly what it is ...*

epilogue

Ana apologized profusely when I called her, saying she would never forgive herself for putting me in that situation. I told her I had one request, that she release it now, and so would I, as it was a gift meant to serve us both. I then inquired deeper about what might have caused it. Ana said that she was diagnosed with anxiety disorder as a child, and had gone to a lot of therapy, always believing something was wrong with her.

She said she had changed so much by doing the SOS practices that she didn't feel like the same person, and couldn't live with that *story* anymore. She said she struggled for quite some time, but in the end felt it was the right thing to do. Hearing her speak of the many difficulties she transcended made me grateful for what is possible for us all. Surely, this is what it meant by that beautiful saying, 'and the truth will set you free'.

THINKING, SPEAKING & TRANSMITTING

There is a remarkably powerful technology just waiting to be presented to humanity. And, it's not a futuristic computer system ...

IT IS YOU

While we each have the capability to transmit higher states of consciousness,[1] many more people today are unfortunately sending out lower-density emissions of frustration, conflict, pride and blame. There are over 60,000 thoughts running through your mind each day, and a large part of them are conditioned impulses; reactive and negative thoughts that dominate and cloud your responses.

We all have triggers that go off within us – learning how to change this 'environment' of unconscious thoughts and words makes a crucial difference in each day. Our nerves are biological electrical conductors that transmit information from the brain to all the parts of our body. For your body to make better chemicals that support more productive uplifting thoughts, the messages need to resonate with higher states of consciousness.

Repeating 'happy words" is helpful, but they can't eliminate the density of the emotional blockage and patterns that cause these self-defeating conversations in your head. Some are those you might not even be aware of – as they are buried deep where ancestral conditioning and stress exist.

223

Connection with the unwavering Energy of coherence accelerates the natural healing process that releases this density – and, your focused attention on the process takes the experience from being one of a leisurely walk in the park, to a ride on a NASCAR/Formula 1 track. Your participation ignites consistent purification, and the awareness that brings lasting change.

your impact on the listening cells in your body as well as the world around you

For years we have believed that most unwritten communication was thinking and speaking. Now, we need to add a third element to this equation – *transmitting*. Scientific research has demonstrated how the thoughts we think and the words we speak have a direct influence on our health and the quality of our lives.[2] We know now that the body's 37.2 trillion cells are listening and[3] many are responding. You have the capability to rewire the brain to make better choices and bring your body into a natural flow of healthy renewal and harmony – and the opposite is true as well. Thank goodness these responses don't manifest that rapidly or we might all be even more stressed!

What we haven't fully realized is the extraordinary potential we have to turn this around; consider the phenomenal impact you can have by *transmitting* frequencies of higher consciousness! When you are happy or content you already broadcast optimism, and that is why people you are with begin shifting toward your emotional state. Increasing the dynamic of your Energetic intelligence accelerates this ability immensely (*see Step Over That Line, Flights of Hope and Promise*) and what you find is that less and less time is spent listening to thoughts and speaking words that don't uplift you.

What you transmit through your thoughts and emotions can bring people in close proximity into a corresponding vibration; this occurs by the 'driver' of the frequency playing the loudest note (uplifting or depressing). Imagine how bright a room would be lit if every person who entered was like a high-wattage bulb, rather than a room full of people with mini flashlights, or candles with flickering flames.

I am speaking metaphorically of course as the science of how this all occurs can seem so complex it makes the mind spin endlessly. Therefore I included even more research as well as videos on the CONNECT pages, where you can dive as deep as you like. What is most important to understand is taking responsibility for what *you* are sending out *and* how to magnify your impact.

a new perspective on 'communication' is opening

The latest scientific discoveries about water offer impressive documentation that could also shift your perception about the effects of communication. Recent discoveries have proven that water is capable of storing and recording information. Water receives the imprint of outside influences, much as we do, remembers it, and then stores it like a computer. Dr. Konstantin Korotkov, from the National Research University of Russia, reported after considerable experimentation, that positive and negative human emotions had extensive influence on water's memory. Since 70–90 percent of our bodies are made of water, it is safe to assume that the intelligent information centers in the body are listening and recording the emotional content of what is communicated.[4]

transmitting intelligent energy

The first time I physically experienced this dynamic Energy that has the power to immediately shift your perspective on life, it was transmitted from a master of meditation visiting from the East.[5] I was standing in a long line of people waiting to meet him, and I suddenly felt a strong energetic pulsation in my body. I looked around, wondering what could have elicited such an unusual sensation. As I got closer to the teacher, that feeling became stronger, to the point of nausea, and I eventually had to race to the nearest bathroom. My body began to detoxify from the impurities I had placed in it over the years. I'm sure now it was also cleansing the traumatic memories in my cells, as I considered, for the first time, forgiving my father. Within a month, I had released enough chemical imbalance that I was able to let go a ten-year cocaine habit. It was a turning point as my awareness accelerated as well, and I discovered more happiness coming into my life in the weeks and months to follow.

Did this teacher realize I needed help, or did the Energy field he emitted very naturally impact me and each person standing in that line who was ready to move into higher consciousness? David R. Hawkins, M.D., PhD, was the first 'average' person I became aware of who had the ability to transmit an Energy field that has this level of impact.[1]

In *Power vs. Force* he wrote about one event where he could feel it being transmitted to a street gang about to fight, who ended up laughing instead.[6] It would move through him without his even having to think about it. He spoke of phenomena like this occurring as a consequence of the power of the field itself, and that it is impersonal, i.e. you, just being you, can become a transducer of this phenomenal power, by allowing it to flow through you.

you, fully empowered, transmit higher consciousness

Throughout history the capacity to transmit Energy that raised consciousness was considered a rare gift, available to only very few people. This capacity is available now to everyone who opens and prepares for this possibility. Becoming coherent is essential. It is not a parlor trick, or magic, even though it can bring about miraculous events. It's about extending empowerment. And, it begins by connecting, and allowing this exquisitely powerful field of Love to flow through you.

Dr. Hawkins understood; he lived his life, not as a healer or an 'enlightened master', *but simply to uplift consciousness while working at his chosen career*. This is what the future can look like – people in all walks of life transmitting super-awareness, living and accessing the ever-evolving potential of humanity.

You can transmit different forms of *communication* that bring people into higher consciousness by just being you. What this advanced life Energy instills is the ability to be compassionate, inclusive and purposeful, and to seek actions that are solution oriented. Transmitting Conscious Communication develops this capability organically over time. What you will find as you read about the people in this section is how they discovered these abilities appearing in their lives as they attuned to it through consistent practice.

transducers of true potential

When you are in connection to your highest potential, you are accessing information that exists beyond the conditioned mind – and, you have the capability to send it out. Dr. William Tiller states in his latest book, "Subtle energies are real energies that are not directly observable because they function at the level of the vacuum. They can be converted to an observable and our present human condition only via an intermediate transducer. Today these transducers are primarily living systems."[7]

YOU are that living system! And, your understanding of this ignites a greater recognition of your self-worth and true potential. What you transmit makes a difference. Dr. David Hawkins states it this way: "... it is the formless that accompanies the form of words which accounts for the transmission. The same words, spoken as mere intellectual learning, lack the power of the carrier wave that facilitates the comprehension by the listener. Words transmitted with power bring about transformation in the listener."

As you spend more time communicating consciously, you will notice how connection with the unwavering Energy of coherence changes your perception of yourself. New beliefs accelerate the natural healing process that streams through the cellular structure of the body and the neural pathways in your brain. Communicating consciously accelerates all forms of learning and therapy by coupling it with a river of intelligence that works on the cellular level where lasting change occurs.

Regardless of how you communicate today, your inner and outer conversations can rapidly shift and, as they do, what you'll notice is how your environment changes to mirror the powerfully loving state you now transmit.

SUPER COOL ...
SELENA'S NEW LIFE

Blue hairstreaks and towering high heels, Selena was a *super cool* Latina stylist at a happening hair salon in Santa Monica. She was living life in the fast lane, as so many do today, out drinking with friends several nights a week, and running on empty. When I arrived for my third appointment, she was so much larger than when we first met, I politely inquired how she was doing. She told me about an unbearable pain in her back and legs. The diagnosis at the hospital was *erythema nodosum*, an inflammation of the skin that's so debilitating it soon became difficult for her to even walk.

Selena now had a weekly appointment at the hospital to check her blood, and when needed she would join the others hooked up to machines that drained the excess fluid from their body. The doctors had prescribed a host of medications, and she was retaining enormous amounts of water as a result. Selena had been told there was no cure; that she would have to live with this disease her entire life. She had just turned 26.

I invited her to attend a program and tried to explain how this advanced life Energy was affecting people's health and lives. I had only recently left my previous vocation and it was challenging for me to communicate the wondrous effects without sounding slightly 'off center'. Selena's unvarnished response communicated exactly how she felt, "I don't believe in anything like that. I'll be just fine ... really." Her smile said it all, *Thanks ... but nooo thanks!*

When I returned the next month Selena's body was even larger, and her life had become more difficult. Standing on swollen legs with an aching back all day was taking its toll on her mentally and physically. This hard-working, fun-loving woman was becoming seriously depressed. She was taking a lot of medication, and the weekly hospital visits consistently reminded her of the life she no longer lived. I asked her again – this time, she said yes.

waking up is not that hard to do

"Have you noticed anything different?" It was a couple of days after the program. I wanted her to spend a moment in reflection, as the subtleties of the experience can happen for some so quietly that you could miss the messages that appear if you're not looking. A smile came across her face. "Come to think of it, something did happen. It usually takes me about 45 minutes to get to work and I get *road rage* at all the crazies out there – but the very next day when I got in my car, I suddenly found a talk radio show that was so funny I laughed all the way to work! The doctors think my sickness is stress related, so laughing is good for me. Yeah ... that was pretty cool."

What appears as synchronicity is one way new insight is delivered as your energetic field shifts from anxiety to possibility and trust. Very organically, Selena's life began to improve. Imagine the difference it could make if instead of spending hours a day screaming at people from your car – you were flexible and could flow with whatever comes up. Selena was more relaxed than I'd ever seen her. "Now I laugh all the way to work. Isn't that great?!"

New awareness began to permeate every area of her life. No longer in reaction, Selena's changing perspective participated in the design of it, guided by *inner conversations* of what would be in her best interest. Her resistance to new ideas had diminished to such an extent, she embraced whatever appeared – even big changes she didn't see coming.

Within a few months she left the salon and found a different environment where she liked the people more and didn't feel the same stress. When her boyfriend got an eviction notice that their apartment building had been sold, Selena wasn't even upset. She took it in her stride and began searching for a new place. "I found one that's even better than where I was! There's more light, it's happier."

The Universe was conspiring to give Selena a new life. Anything that didn't support her in finding balance just began to shut down. A workout studio opened nearby; Selena liked it so much she joined an exercise boot camp. Her body got stronger and the weight began to drop off. She made new choices that surprised even her. She no longer had three drinks at the bar with friends, but one or two, and would leave early. Nutritious foods became appealing and fried foods began disappearing as her body naturally craved what matched her new lifestyle.

transmitting towers of healing energy

Each time I came for my hair appointment that Energy force would heighten, streaming waves of healing to Selena. Talking about the practical aspects of life, she learned the SOS Tools that would translate into the conscious habits she soon developed. Each time we visited, it was clear to see how she had incorporated these tools into her life. The knee-jerk reactions, the rage and the cynicism seemed to have all dissipated – while she still retained the sharp wit and fun personality that was always her trademark.

The world-weary young woman I originally met became a powerhouse of strength who transmitted her light to everyone she met. The *wild child* became a mainstay of support for her family and friends in ways that were unexplainable even to her. Selena was now the one they turned to for love and guidance. Her journey into illness contributed to an immense compassion and when her 11-year-old niece was diagnosed with leukemia, Selena was by her side, week after week. Her presence helped to calm her niece in ways no one else could, and she was able to help and guide her, to the very moment of her passing. We are all catalysts and messengers, transmitters of love and kindness, or pessimism and rage. Not only through the words we speak but communicated invisibly through energetic waves. As we become more in tune, this love reaches wider and wider circles of influence, resonating into the very heart of humankind.

empowerment lives within you

Selena became physically and mentally stronger day by day, month by month, and it happened naturally. The integration of this advanced Energy with the tools that empowered her life choices converged and brought Selena all that was needed for indelible change. This pint-sized chica became so in tune with her body that she knew instinctively when she was pushing too hard, and would immediately slow down, breathe deep and connect with the intelligence that was sending her inspired guidance.

Selena began to question why she needed the same amount of medication she'd been given when originally diagnosed, as she was feeling so well. One day she told her doctors that she would like to begin paring down her daily medication. They didn't agree, insisting *she had to face facts – she had a life-long illness and nothing would change that*.

The choices Selena made in the months ahead were made by a woman who wanted to participate in her wellbeing. She wanted to work *with* the doctors, *and* she didn't want to take prescription drugs if they weren't needed. Each month she took fewer pills and observed if her body would stay balanced. When she reached the six-month celebration of being healthy without taking *any* medication, she went for her usual testing.

It was at this time the doctors told her they might have *misdiagnosed her illness, as they couldn't find a trace of the disease in her body*.

In *Spontaneous Evolution*, Bruce Lipton comments on how healing can occur when an individual consciously or even unconsciously makes a significant change in their beliefs and behaviors.[1] For Selena, that choice began by simply saying yes to an invitation that would impact her journey of empowerment – to live in a way that was no longer life threatening, but life enhancing ... how very cool is that.

INSIGHTS, QUESTIONS & REFLECTIONS

How is Selena's health today? Selena is well today, almost 12 years later. The "lifelong illness" she was diagnosed with has not returned.

How is it possible that someone living a lifestyle like Selena's can change their habits? The SOS Tools are made to put a directed focus on what you want to see leave you, and what you want to develop – and to do it in a way that is very organic to the way you live. I didn't tell Selena to change anything, I taught her the tools; from setting Intentions, to Making Requests, from Transmitting Conscious Communication to Release & Let Go. They made sense to her, so she used them. As the Energy field transmitted from the program and our visits – expanded her capabilities, she began responding to life by not reacting, and by becoming still and acting from inspiration instead. As she applied this life practice, it shifted her lifestyle. And soon, she had a new home, new job and improved health.

If someone is ill or having difficulty in their lives, can anyone become a 'transmitting tower' to help them? You are always transmitting your energetic state. If you are feeling love and compassion, it can be experienced by those around you. And, the more you connect to the unified field, releasing whatever blocks you have, that life force will continue to magnify what you transmit. Each person opens to what is best for them; simply being a transmitting tower of higher consciousness, of Love and peace, without expectation is a wonderful gift you offer yourself and others.

DNA research has evidenced that energetic frequencies move through words – how was Selena affected by this? When you are in the presence of this Energy stream, whether it is moving through any of the formats that SOS has developed; recordings of music and words, books, or live presentations, you are immersed in that invisible Energetic force field. *The New Science, Part 3,* explains this through DNA, and Subtle Energies. We all have the capability to transmit the higher frequencies of healing and love. As Selena's vibration changed, her way of communicating changed as well, and it became apparent to everyone – even her family members related to her differently. People began coming to Selena for advice – this was something that had never happened before. They now felt the loving nature that was always there but not previously evident.

If someone doesn't want to change their lifestyle, can SOS still help them? Selena didn't take very good care of herself, and was running on empty. She was living *la vida loca* (a crazy life) and wasn't interested in changing it in any way. After the first program, when she learned The SOS Method, her way of living and being shifted very organically; she didn't have to cut out drinking alcohol, she just naturally cut back. She didn't have to force herself to stop eating greasy foods, she just naturally wanted healthier food.

If a person begins just by applying any of the SOS Tools and Technology, their detrimental lifestyle will eventually dissipate. As you develop a simple practice of bringing the Energy of consciousness into your life, the patterns that don't support a healthy lifestyle will slowly drop away. What you get is a lot more than what you might think you are letting go of.

ROCK N ROLL, DRUGS & HIGHER LEARNING

Tattooed arms and a nose ring gave him the unmistakable look of a wanna-be LA musician. Jeffrey, the teenage son of a friend, needed a job, so he began working in the SOS offices as a transcriber of audio courses. One day when passing by I noticed him peering into the computer, eyes glazed, as though lost in some other time or dimension.

The following week he stood at my door, politely introduced himself, and asked if I had a moment to hear about the mysterious events that had occurred since beginning work – those that had crystallized his recent confusion. He talked about an energy that raced through his body on his first day while listening to the SOS Course audio. And how he became aware after that experience of the enormous anger he had.

Jeffrey felt his mother was treating him unfairly, and decided he'd had enough. So he *told his mother off*, and then added his girlfriend to the list. When that didn't make him feel any better, he looked deeper. There were many things that troubled Jeffrey, one being that he hadn't figured out what he wanted to do with his life. He suddenly understood that he wasn't upset with his mom, he was upset with himself, so he took her to lunch, apologized and then repaired the relationship with his girlfriend.

Soon after that, everything completely changed. Jeffrey became infused with a vitality and inspiration that was now igniting his days with a new passion for life. He told me

I had really hit on something great with this *Stillness thing* and that I should figure out a way for it to be taught in school, "I never learned anything in school that helped me see more clearly than this!" This young man's journey of connecting to his potential had clearly been boosted into high gear.

Enthusiasm poured out of him, igniting a whole new way of communicating that was slightly uncommon for someone who had appeared to be so low key. "I can't believe how energized I am. All the things that I've ever wanted to do and never had the energy for – I'm finally doing them now and it feels great!"

Ageless at 19, he was bright, articulate and filled with curiosity. Whatever he communicated in SOS courses would always be memorable, and would assist people to understand the many changes that occur when you've embarked on an adventure as extraordinary as getting to know your very soul.

the spiral down

Life's evolutionary dance took Jeffrey into many new arenas in the years that followed. I learned that he had fallen in love and was living in New Mexico. Jeffrey had made that big move out of his mom's house and into a whole new life. I would hear good news about him from time to time, until the day his mother called with concern – all communication had stopped. The adventures her son was now discovering are those as a parent you wish would never happen. The following is how it was relayed to me – the pain, as well as the passion of Jeffrey's remarkable journey:

Feelings of hopelessness wracked his body as tears fell on the grimy carpet where he lay. Partying, drinking and snorting endless rounds of cocaine. Not eating, rarely sleeping and hanging out with pseudo-friends. His internal cries of abandonment were like the howls of a trapped animal who has relinquished all hope of ever being saved. A voice responded from the inner depths, echoing a plea of remembrance, *You just think you can't get out because you're so deep in … it's not true* … Jeffrey's cry for help echoed through the uncaring walls of his bare apartment, "*What should I do?*"

Echoes of the *knowing* that would always guide him at his most vulnerable moments surfaced in the midst of his darkest hour, letting him know that he didn't have to do this anymore, that there was a way out … that he could turn it around.

Jeffrey recalled a memory when I spoke about how I had made it through my challenges with drugs and alcohol. Then he remembered the peace he always felt in Stillness Sessions – and how much he needed to feel that way again. The path ahead became clear, he knew the way back.

the spiral up

The next night Jeffrey sat next to a stranger in a bar, who was destined to become a friend. His intention for that new life directed his words and actions. Jeffrey let go of all pretenses, and communicated from his heart why it was important to walk away from his current job and relationship. A week later, that same person called to say she had just been hired as the head chef in a top restaurant and wanted to know if he would like a job. It was a signpost called forth from the field of all potential he had set with his Intention, clarifying the next step in his life journey.

Jeffrey had wanted to have a career that would align him with the man he knew he was. In the months ahead, as he reclaimed the practices that had always inspired him, his spirits lifted, and a passion emerged to attend culinary school. How it would happen wasn't clear, and that was okay with him. He was happy, he was working, and he was off drugs. He loved the people at the restaurant – and they loved him, the ones he worked with as well as the customers that returned again and again, not only for the great food, but to spend time with the man he had become.

The day I visited the restaurant, it was easy to see why he was so popular. His smile reached from one side of his face to the other as he lifted me off my feet with a welcome that resonated from the depth of his heart. Each person that entered received that same genuine sense of caring that seemed to flow so naturally out of him. Somehow, all that had happened to Jeffrey had brought him to a place of greater love and compassion, and now it was being transmitted through an enthusiasm that literally lit the entire restaurant.

Sometimes a walk on the wild side, through internal challenges you would never choose, can bring new strengths and purpose to your entire life – and the gifts it brings are those that can last a lifetime.

INSIGHTS, QUESTIONS & REFLECTIONS

Did Jeffrey stay off drugs? Jeffrey is living a drug-free life. He learned all he could in the three years he apprenticed at the restaurant, and eventually moved to another city to make the needed finances for studying at a culinary school. He has set his sights on having a restaurant of his own and is working toward that now.

How did changing the 'conversations' in his thoughts and words assist him in changing his life? When he remembered how the practices of SOS had helped him before, and went back to them, it shifted his inner and outer communication. He let go of people that didn't match his new life, including the girlfriend who was still doing drugs. Within 24 hours he connected with people who were headed in this new direction, the chef and those at the restaurant. As he began to transmit new inner and outer communication that reflected his new outlook, life began to change.

Cocaine's addictive qualities can make it extremely tough to get 'clean'. Is it possible someone can stop without being in a 'program'? What is key is dissolving blocks on a cellular level. As imprints from past memory are eliminated from the body through contact with higher healing frequencies, you are able to move into a state of coherence, of harmony. When there is a lowering of energy from illness, stress and emotional overload, your body needs assistance to get into that natural flow. SOS clears out patterns that might otherwise live on from our past – recent and generational – and this can happen rapidly, as it did for the women in upstate New York (*see Prelude*) and over time as it did for Jeffrey. And, as stated earlier, it will be different for each person as we each have levels of generational patterns that need releasing.

Is it possible to change your life and not return to destructive patterns? Each time you practice Stillness Sessions it activates this healing Energy to expand within you, and your practice of the SOS Tools develops new conscious habits. These tools can become your *program*; they are used by many people today who have released addictions. If you don't include the practices that make your body fit and strong, by going to a gym, walking, swimming, or any number of activities, your body will have a difficult time staying well and could actually become quite unhealthy. *This is why including SOS as an ongoing practice is so helpful.* As you shift on all three levels – body, mind and spirit – your past patterns no longer call out to you and new ones are developed in your neural pathways through the many positive experiences that occur.

What gave Jeffrey the energy and excitement he spoke of? The body naturally makes chemicals; dopamine and serotonin are two well-known neurotransmitters that create a euphoric high. Two theories of how this occurs are:

1. The Energy stream transmitted immediately begins clearing blockages so the person's natural chemical production (of serotonin and/or dopamine) activates,

giving them a sampling of what their natural state is – and could be once more.

2. The Energy stream ignites a natural high, the quality of which is a new sensory experience that occurs as the person begins to vibrate on this higher frequency. (Similar to the tuning fork theory.)[1]

In Dr. Gabor Mate's book, *In The Realm of Hungry Ghosts*, there are many references to research done on the effects of cocaine, nicotine, crystal meth, over-eating and sex, as well as prescription drugs – and what they do to inhibit the uptake of messenger molecules including serotonin and dopamine.[2] "On the cellular level, addiction is all about neurotransmitters and their receptors."

Human beings seem to actively look for stimulants to relieve the stress of life. Dopamine gives you incentive, vitality, curiosity and feel-good optimism – which you can get from a natural high when this Energy field activates *your own* biochemistry.

What ignited Jeffrey's initial awareness of his anger when listening to SOS course audio? Subtle energies are transmitted through various formats, coupled on sound frequency, in course and program audio recordings as well as Stillness Sessions. How this is possible is clarified through what the latest research is reporting regarding sound and word frequencies (*see DNA, Part 3*).

Why did Jeffrey 'forget' what he had learned – his studies in higher knowledge – and then get into drugs? Each person has a life journey that guides them to their innate potential, which could have some crossroads, that are challenging but can be ultimately beneficial. Consider how this 'downturn' brought Jeffrey to meet many new people – to apprentice in a restaurant, and to discover what he wanted to do with his life, i.e. to be a chef. This might not have happened otherwise. And, his journey brought him tremendous empowerment. Now, he is clear on what fuels his life, and how applying practices that make it work – work.

How did having conscious communication make a difference, and how did it happen? Jeffrey's commitment to a different life supported the new conversations in his head that were no longer self-destructive. As he started using the SOS Tools that heightened his focus, his thoughts reflected the new direction he was headed. By activating the potential he set new events in motion, thereby meeting the chef. As he began communicating kindness and optimism, it resonated out from him, bringing totally different circumstances into his life.

PS. Jeffrey recently got married. Life is looking pretty good these days.

TRANSMITTING CONSCIOUS COMMUNICATION
why, when, what & how

All communication is a transmission of something broadcast, conveyed, or circulated. You are like a 'transmitting tower' broadcasting 24/7 to everyone around you, including the intelligent cells in your body. Becoming aware of your communication – your thoughts, as well as the words you speak – impacts you on a mental, emotional and physiological level. Attuning your energetic frequency is everything toward having a quality of life that generates loving relationships, prosperity and purpose.

Why is Transmitting Conscious Communication important to me? Choosing thoughts and words that match your intended 'state' immediately elevates your state of mind and frequency. It's not about repeating empty words that don't ring true. This is where affirmations can be off mark. While they can support you by reminding you of what you intend, if your inner conversations are not resonating that higher frequency, then affirming words will not be very effective. Connecting to the intelligent healing Energy that releases old patterns so you resonate on higher levels with the conscious thoughts and words you think and speak is key.

It also ignites the transmitters in your brain to be rewired and function in a way that develops new behavior and actions. Elevated emotions of love, appreciation, and happiness support your entry into even higher frequencies that bring healing and empowerment into every area of life.

As your awareness grows and communication begins to shift, it brings a release of restrictive feelings. The new *environment* Transmitting Conscious Communication creates resonates through the intelligent cellular structure of your mind and body. You feel vital, hopeful and more alive. Your life begins to mirror the expanded joy, health and awareness you transmit into the world around you.

When should I apply Transmitting Conscious Communication? Any thoughts, words and actions that reflect anger, aggression, worry, grief, shame or guilt have an enormously detrimental impact on your productivity, state of mind and health. Imagine the difference it would make if you communicated in a way that fully empowered you and every person you encountered. Language, words and their sound frequency have a tremendous impact on your DNA (*see Part 3*) – it's not just about speaking kinder words. The next level of this understanding is evolutionary – it includes the third element – transmitting – that changes everything:

THINKING, SPEAKING ... & TRANSMITTING

The vibrational difference in what you communicate affects your emotional state, the cellular structure in your body, and your evolutionary path to higher consciousness. Let's start with words – as they express an energy field and engender whatever meaning you give them:

LISTEN to how these words sound and feel: **hopeless, cynical, calculating, opinionated, intimidating, condemning, resentful, rigid, hateful.** Words that resonate fear and disappointment will affect you adversely as you communicate aloud or activate them through your actions.

LISTEN to the difference of the frequency in these words, how they sound and feel: **considerate, kindness, flexibility, willingness, generosity, friendly, gracious, illuminating, gratitude, acceptance, beauty, love.** It's easy to notice the difference, isn't it?

Now consider the energy you transmit. Since you are a transducer,[1] consistently sending and receiving energy, the influence of what you send out through your energetic field is affecting your mental, emotional and physiological state as well as that of those around you. This becomes the epigenetic environment that not only impacts you in this lifetime, but generations to come (*see Epigenetics, Part 3*). Transmitting Conscious Communication is a tool you can return to again and again to continually vitalize your inner and outer communication. As you do, you bring higher consciousness into the world and support others to live the empowered life you now have.

SPECIAL TIP: Begin exactly where you are. Each time you hear yourself saying a word that doesn't match your intention, you can replace it in that moment. What you will find is that it immediately shifts your emotional state, and before long, the pattern is naturally eliminated and a new habit is formed.

When your thoughts and words are kind and caring, you send out electromagnetic waves that continue to elevate you as well as those around you – this again is not just about saying words that don't match the 'background' of your emotional content – it's about attuning every part of you to higher frequencies.

SOS TOOL: TRANSMITTING CONSCIOUS COMMUNICATION

1 APPLY TOOL & TEACHING:
a. **Explore**/review SOS Teaching.
b. **Reflect with Three Breath Awareness** on the commitment to transform your communication; thoughts, words and what you energetically transmit.
c. **Write** what doesn't work today – and what you intend to communicate and transmit beginning now.

2 ACTIVATE ENERGY POTENTIAL THROUGH STILLNESS SESSIONS TECHNOLOGY:
a. **Listen** to a *Sacred Word* Session, simply listen or repeat the words with intent and feeling once or more a day. You can also listen and speak the words of an *Elevate Session* at anytime in the week ahead.

3 ACT ON INSPIRATION AS IT IS REVEALED:
a. **Replace** lower frequency words throughout the day.
b. **Replace** lower frequency thoughts; by thinking or saying, *"Thank you. I love you."* This seemingly simple phrase has a remarkably powerful and immediate effect. Try it now to see how it makes you feel, then use it to elevate your frequency anytime ... and just smile.

c. **Write** what happens during the week in your journal. Notice how it shifts the way you feel, what you transmit and the way others respond to you.

Including this SOS Tool escalates your journey into healing and living from your highest potential; as existing blocks are released and conscious awareness expands you send out waves of higher value. During the coming days and always, transmit respect and love to yourself and to everyone. Observe how your empowerment translates through the events appearing in your life.

SETTING
POTENT INTENTIONS
the potency factor

What's at stake is your entire life. If you aren't aiming at what you want your life to be about, you are just managing whatever shows up ... day after day, year after year. Intention creates a context for your life in this moment and in the future: what you value, who you see yourself to be, and what you believe is possible.

Intentions have different levels of potency. When an Intention is highly focused, and is *coupled* with the Energy sea of potential (Stillness Sessions Technology), it has the organizing power to set circumstances and events in motion that increase your overall influence and enjoyment of life. Setting a Potent Intention gives you more evidence of your power to attune with the joy of creation.

The quality of your Intentions, when inspired by higher awareness, develops and sustains a life you love – from meaningful work, to loving relationships, from having a healthy body to deep, sacred experiences.

EVEN ELUSIVE DREAMS CAN COME TRUE

"I've worked hard for this. I don't understand how they can even ask me! What am I supposed to do?" His words were like the anguished cry of a battle-weary peacekeeper, watching his dreams slowly and surely slip into mists of oblivion. My cynical, intellectual, often arrogant, yet endearing, and always good-hearted friend was really up against it now.

Jake had chosen to set his latest aspirations on producing an *impossibly challenging* documentary, a story of great strength and stamina, owned by an equally powerful and strong-willed man. He spent months working without pay to bring this elusive project some reality and had succeeded until, quite unexpectedly, he received an ultimatum to accept a lesser *producing credit* or "... get nothing and just walk away." The smoke and illusion of titles, especially in the domain of Hollywood grandiosity, can create a reality that opens doors to offers and projects where none exist. Jake's outcries were those that arrive from the depth of a man's heart when he believes that he will not be able to play on the field of dreams he knows is his birthright.

show me the money ... or at least the fame

It had been drilled into Jake his whole life that hard work would take him to the top of that ladder of recognition and success, and that putting in endless hours of work would create the results he intended. We've all been there, slaving away when we're not conscious of how to be the authors of our own lives. Many Eastern traditions describe unconsciousness as humanity's inability to see beyond the *veil* – that thin layer of deception that holds Truth just beyond sight – where we have forgotten our inherent *knowing*, our ability to create life from the Energy sea of pure potential.

the game changer

What to do? Jake thought *that title* would create his dreams – that was another illusion. "What do you *really* want?" I asked, inviting him to look deeper at the overall intention he had set for his life purpose. Jake's fervent response was, "I want to make films that touch people's hearts to recognize their humanity." His passion suddenly shifted to anger, "*And* I want my title! I earned it! Why should I give it up?!" His words reverberated the indignity he felt.

Jake's outburst shifted from rage to an enduring cry, imploring the intelligence of this universe to show the way. "*What can I do?!*"

"Will the film get made if you insist on keeping your title?"

"No." The only thing Jake could see in this moment was righteous anger and defeat. He had earned the right to be the producer. Yet, if he fought to keep the title, his life would become mired in waging a war of endless battles.

seeing what you can't, trusting what you can

Jake couldn't see it, but a bigger vision was unfolding that was in complete alignment with his vision. When you can let go of beliefs that bind you and trust that what you have envisioned is unfolding – what appears is beyond your imagination. Infinite intelligence will reveal the underlying principles of form into matter; thoughts manifesting into events. This equation was evidenced rapidly when answers to Jake's questions surfaced that night. Embittered states were left behind, answers were received, and limitations that had been thought real were dissolved.

As the Stillness Session recording in the program resonated the infinite potential that propels your journey, Jake had a vision of himself as a young child longing for his father's love and approval. He saw a time when his father knocked him unconscious – right off his chair in the dining room. Jake watched the child who wanted assurance that he was *worthy* of being loved, return again and again to his father, silently asking for that message of security and comfort. He never got it.

What he could see now were the many ways this brokenhearted child kept looking for that love, in one situation after the next, throughout his entire life. He suddenly realized he didn't have to look any further. Welling up inside him was a cry of liberation, "I *already* have the love I've always wanted ... I *am* that love." Beneath the fractured layers of loss and grief, what his vision uncovered brought him a new resolve.

Words are a form of *illumination* not only by what they express, but also through the vibrational content of the energy field they transmit. What Jake shared opened the heart of everyone who heard it. The room resounded in sacred Stillness, the kind you hear in inner sanctums where whispered prayers echo a call to God. This power exists when absolute Love pulsates through you – even your mind won't be able to question what you experience when it's as palpable as what this force emits. This state of consciousness allows you to let go, ever so gently, of anything that has blocked you. The immeasurable Energy that streams forth is what generates improbable dreams into existence.

working harder ... is not always smarter

What you intend is greatly impacted by accessing this field of potential, this pulsing Energy stream of life. It's not about stressing, or working harder. It's about taking action from the inspiration that arrives as these points of attraction, intention and energy potential coalesce. Another gift this knowledge ignites is that you become happy with what you *already* have. So you play the game, no longer feeling anxious, but rather as a way to take responsibility for your life, seeing it as an exploration into greater discoveries.

In a moment of recognition, the newly enlightened producer was given everything he needed to make the decision. Jake released the beliefs that had bound his situation in despair, called the film's director and relinquished the title that had once held so much meaning.

Within 24 hours the quantum field began to create the impossible. The director was so impressed with the courage it had taken for Jake to let go of his position after all he had done to get the film made, that he recommended him to a filmmaker who had just lost her producer. The director suggested she do everything in her power to hire him. He told her how fortunate she would be to work with a person who had a level of integrity not often found in a business where deceit and despair live like brothers from the same family.

He tried to act low key when he called, but the euphoria in his voice was indicative of the news he had to share. He got the job! Jake was booked on a flight for Africa, leaving in just two weeks to produce a film he was deeply passionate about. And, it had that elusive title. He would be credited as the producer!

Jake's overall vision was a match to this new situation he now found himself in as the film was a declaration of hope and inspiration in a sea of uncertainty, a penetrating perspective of mortality and transcendence. It was a documentary about children with difficulties most of us will never have to face – living without parents, without knowing they are loved, and living with the reality their days are numbered from the disease of AIDS.

Jake gave these kids all the love that was now pouring out of him. He gave them the love that he had always wanted – and they gave it right back.

Beyond what fame and fortune can ever offer, what Jake received was the richest gift of all – the awareness at the depth of your being that you are loved. So much opens in your life when you *really* get this. Now, the titles could arrive as well as the money. It's just the way it is.

Jake won numerous awards in the years ahead, including the highest accolades possible from Amnesty International. His life began to model what had once only been an elusive dream. What resonated within him now produced more films of a world united by love for all humanity. This was only the first of the films he made that would speak to this awareness in the years ahead. What more could you want than that? If one day you see Jake's smiling face receiving an Oscar, you can smile right back, as you now know the road there and how to take it for yourself.

ADDING POTENCY TO HIGHLY FOCUSED THOUGHTS

Intentions have become somewhat 'mainstream' – more and more people today seem to understand how useful they can be. But has their impact become watered down? Have they become words on a page, or momentary thoughts that don't carry the influence they can have when practiced in a way that develops their potency?

A few years back, mission statements became popular through Stephen Covey's book, *The 7 Habits of Highly Effective People*.[1] It took off like wildfire; suddenly people everywhere had an awareness of what could galvanize positive forward motion. Everyone wanted it, whether for a large or small company, or setting your own personal compass. It was a huge step forward in unifying vision and purpose with value – and what was discovered over time is that these inspirational and encouraging words weren't very impactful if they hadn't been woven into the structure of the company, or integrated into the life of the individual.

Thoughts and words are the initial ingredients to create the circumstances that form your life's journey. When activated by the energetic field of potential – the potency increases exponentially. This is why you always want to couple your Intentions with the Stillness Session Technology, where the subtle energies transmitted increase the effects of this organizing principle to bring events and circumstances into reality. Simply adding even a five-minute audio recording makes a marked difference.

energy, frequencies and vibration

The very fabric of this universe is matter and energy – and all *matter* (atoms and molecules) consists of energetic frequencies in motion. Nicola Tesla, one of the most gifted scientists and inventors of the modern age, whose inventions harnessed the power of atoms and electrons, wrote, "If you want to find the secrets of the universe, think in terms of energy, frequencies and vibration."[2]

enhancing your creative power

"Every Intention is an act of creation."[3] Knowing this, how are you using this extraordinary ability? Intentions are thoughts and words that have an energetic frequency, which resonates through your *inner and outer communication*. What you are thinking subconsciously, if it resonates frequencies of doubt or concern, has an influence on the intention you have set. It's like repeating affirmations of 'life being perfect' when you're really feeling depressed – it's just not very effective. The opposite is also true – when you are resonating on higher levels of consciousness attuned to flexibility, inspiration and enthusiasm – the frequency of *you*, and your words and thoughts fully support your Intentions.

When you consider that your choices, behavior and actions are initiated first by your thoughts, it becomes clear how they participate in creating your life; therefore, setting Intentions that are highly focused with the potency of the organizing field (subtle energies), will have even greater impact in creating a future you love. This is why it's an important practice to understand on the many levels that science is now proving.

the magnifying power of potential

"For the last four hundred years, an unstated assumption of science is that human intention cannot affect what we call 'physical reality'. Our experimental research of the past decade shows that, for today's world and under the right conditions, this assumption is no longer correct.

"We humans are much more than we think we are and Psychoenergetic Science continues to expand the proof of it."[4] Dr. Tiller's intention to amplify humanity's understanding set the tone for the phenomenal research he has evidenced that is lighting a path today and will continue for years to come. His work has brought new understanding of the capabilities of humankind to affect change through Intention. In one recorded study using the IHD (Intention Host Device), specific Intentions broadcast across great distances caused measurable change in autistic children.

The study measured changes in cognitive function, sociability, communication and physical abilities. One fifth-grade child who was initially functioning at a kindergarten level, within ten months was at a fifth-grade level. While many became more physically interactive, one child who had not liked being touched, which is common among the autistic, began asking for hugs.

the phenomenal potency of Intention

Let's review the specifics: Just as medication has different measurements of potency, i.e. 5, 10, 20+ milligrams to get indicated results – Intentions also have different levels of effectiveness. What specifically affects Intention?

What dilutes it? What strengthens it? What causes Intentions to not result in desired outcomes? *A potent Intention is dependent on:*

1. **Your level of focus**
2. **Your inner and outer communication** (frequency)
   - Thoughts and words - harmonious
   - Blocks and patterns – congestion/disharmony
3. **Your activation of Energetic potential** to magnify impact
   a. Connection to unifying field, organizing principle
   b. Elevation of energetic frequency in you
4. **Alignment of Intention with overall life purpose:** look at the big picture (i.e. some intentions might not happen, because you are being guided toward an overall life purpose, and the intention you have set is not the most direct route)

Here again the coherency of The New Science with ancient wisdom and Eastern healing traditions assists in understanding the vibrational frequencies (*see Energy & Awareness*) that set your thoughts in motion and the potency factor. Similar to an unseen matrix in exchange with the quantum sea, The Simplicity of Stillness ignites the higher vibrational states where you access creative potential and inspiration to set a new future in motion.

Intentions ignited by *higher information* change their *quality*; which is of great significance in defining your overall life. When you invite guidance from the *source* of all to inspire your Intentions, and couple them with the exponential Energy that sustains reality – you will create more of life's beauty from that focused power in you.

intention; the playground of your reality

What I personally became aware of when integrating the Setting Potent Intentions tool is how many of my intentions became reality *when in alignment* with the overall purpose of my life's journey. This could clarify for you why you don't get everything you are aiming at, as what you are intending might actually not assist you in the big picture. You can read an example of this in the Story, *Even Elusive Dreams Can Come True*, where Jake didn't get what he originally intended. Once he discovered and released the unconscious beliefs that were blocking the flow of his life purpose being realized, a future that was in harmony with his overall vision appeared.

What this SOS Tool teaches you is how to form a focused intention, and how to remain open, rather than resisting *whatever is happening in the moment*. Rather than listening to any mental tapes that are self-defeating, it teaches you that even when things don't appear to be happening in your best interest – they are. You will learn how to find an inner stillness, to head you in a new direction where an abundance of vitality and enthusiasm await.

I have found that Setting Potent Intentions draws circumstances into my life that I wouldn't have attempted on my own, but in harmony with the universal principle, I have the courage and the insight to play bigger. This has become the norm for many people who use this tool every day. It takes expectations out of the equation, and invites the adventure of life to appear. You are not powerless to what life hands you, but can fully participate in creating it to be all that you have envisioned.

PART 5: Tools, Teachings & Stories

The stories in this section will guide you to set Intentions from the many dreams you are ready to claim. Then all that's left to do is continue walking the journey – keep it simple, and invite the inherent power in you to live the greatest adventure you can imagine, one filled with an abundance of love, prosperity, and connection to what makes it all worthwhile.

THE RELENTLESS PAIN OF BEING A HERO

You could feel the A-type energy he transmitted from the moment he walked in the door. That frenetic kind of juice that seems to pump through the body of those whose job it is to be on high alert 24/7. Ex-marine, firefighter, husband, father, friend. Declared hero in the eyes of many, except for the one who could help him get out of the consuming pain he was in – himself.

When I spoke of my past with drugs and addiction, our eyes connected. And when I got to the part about the intense events that ignited my passion to bring this energetic experiential knowledge to others, he almost smiled. Maybe it was because I likened it to the best high I ever had.

His tattooed body stood out in contrast to most of the people in attendance at the meditative retreat site in the rolling hills of New York where the course was given. While people of every culture and background frequent SOS programs, I wondered what could have made him commit to being at an overnight location such as this. It didn't take long to find out. The plane had been booked for him, as well as the three-day course and accommodations. I wondered if it was a last chance request by a loved one or a prayerful intention?

Dave had always known what he wanted – and he knew what to do to get it. He had been an honor guard at the White House, had served his country in numerous missions overseas, and was considered a hero in every sense of the word. When he returned home after serving his time, Dave landed a great job as a firefighter. Life was good. He had a beautiful wife, a happy, healthy baby, and a great job.

Then suddenly everything went south, nothing seemed to make sense. He couldn't even get to the station, even though he had always enjoyed the job and the guys he worked with. Pacing from room to room, he felt caged without any recourse. Yet something was stopping him, something he couldn't see, but that was clearly there – as it stopped him in his tracks every time he tried to walk out the door. Dave had become a prisoner in his own home.

Why? Why?! He couldn't make any sense of it. Why did he have symptoms of PTSD – the post-traumatic stress so many soldiers and victims of war or violence have? What he had to deal with didn't even compare to the horror some of his buddies had seen. Nothing he could think of that happened should make him feel the searing anguish that his daily life had become. And yet his mind wasn't cooperating.

From one Veterans Hospital to the next, no one's ideas or medications made him feel any better. Life was becoming increasingly difficult. The fact that he didn't even feel connected to his own child or the woman he loved increased the tension, erupting in senseless arguments that continually brought his wife to tears.

Thoughts of suicide began to plague him. How could someone as strong and decisive as he had always been, feel so empty, so useless? In the midst of the drama that was Dave's life, his wife Kathy came across *The Power of Peace in You*, [1] a book describing the process that had healed other people in a way she felt could work for him. That's the beauty of how life works, when as they say, the stars line up. It was my first book.

How does synchronicity like this happen? How did Dave's wife find what could help them at this critical moment in both their lives? When Kathy read what she believed to be an answer to her prayers, she immediately booked everything needed to give Dave a chance to get out of the pain he was in. The power of love, streaming through her intention, and the power of his soul wanting to heal coalesced, bringing together the best circumstances possible. As she said goodbye to the man she loved so dearly, it was with the hope he would find the man he once was, and return to love her again, in the way he once did.

There was a palpable excitement in the air as that stream of Energy resonating through the Stillness Session recording opened the hearts and minds of everyone present. The intention Dave had shared that night, was to find a renewed passion for his life, his work and his family. What became clear to everyone in the room from the moment the music stopped, was that something had happened, and whatever it was – was definitely out of the ordinary.

Like a kid who had just arrived at Disneyland, questions streamed forth with the enthusiasm of curiosity unleashed. In the following days, the force of that power filled Dave with more vitality than he had ever known. The adrenaline rush of war was nothing like this – this was a high that filled him with the passion of life, rather than thoughts of death. It was as if a river of information had reconnected him to what he had known in some lifetime and forgotten. His excitement was palpable, "You just can't ignore an amazing experience like this! It's going to impact my whole life." Little could he imagine how true that statement would be.

Sometimes when people begin the process, they don't fully appreciate how helpful it is to write down your intentions, experiences, the insights and events that happen – not so with Dave. Every time I looked his way, he was scribbling madly, pen in hand like a writer whose muse was pouring information into his head nonstop.

Dave's intention on day one was to heal and it had begun to happen so quickly, he was like a book of empty pages, ready to write a new story that would now become his life. He shared the many difficulties he had faced and those of his friends and family. His heart was bursting with the excitement of someone who has just been unburdened from a tremendous weight. His parting words brought an unexpected sweetness to my heart. "I know so many guys like me, who this could help ... Whatever I can do to help you reach them, let me know ... It's just so unforgettable ..." I can still see his smile even now.

Sometimes you feel like your life is empty, that it has no meaning. I've been there. To find that excitement and passion, that your life is worthwhile, that you can heal from the pain you are in is so very special. What would the world be like if every soldier, wife, child and parent could heal from their mental anguish and return to life with an excitement to begin anew. Just imagine ... Just imagine that ...

INSIGHTS, QUESTIONS & REFLECTIONS

If a person comes to a Simplicity of Stillness program, without initially choosing to be there, will it still work? While I always think it's better to make conscious decisions for whatever you do, this could be another example of what Mary Burmeister, the master teacher of the Eastern healing tradition, had to say in *Ancient Art & The New Science (see Part 1)*,[2] "Must one understand that one's house is being cleaned, or will they simply notice that it has been done?"

The Stillness Session Technology begins working immediately to release the traumatic memories in your cellular body and increase the level of brain chemicals like serotonin that shift your emotional state, i.e. Dave's immediate change in behavior after the first Stillness Session. The changes that occur in the brain and body heal mental, emotional and physical suffering. Healing is an individual process and is different for everyone – *and*, every person who stands in the sunshine, will feel the warmth of the sun.

What caused Dave's breakdown? He wasn't clear what had caused his meltdown. I believe he was reticent to say he had PTSD, as "other guys had experienced much worse in war than I did." What is most important for all the people going through this is the elimination of cellular memory, otherwise, as Dave shared, you could be loaded up with medication, much of which has indications of depression and suicide.

When the mind is conflicted, do we always need to know the source of the pain, or can it be healed without that recognition? Dave's case was unique in that he didn't seem to recognize any direct event that could have blocked him. From the very first time he listened to a Stillness Session where that healing potential ignited, it was clear that somehow – all the lights went on for Dave. He was reflective, joyous, excited and curious.

Emotional pain is individual. Whatever it is for you is meaningful to you. When I initially tried to get over the pain of my father's abuse – I went into analysis, and each time I spoke about it, I got physically ill. When I experienced the harmonious energies of absolute Love that streamed through me when connecting to universal presence, I didn't try to figure it out anymore, just the force of that love began my healing process.

REFLECTION: When you consider that 22 veterans kill themselves every day just in the U.S., and that this number doesn't count the spouses, siblings and parents who commit suicide, the toll of war is inconceivable.[3]

It's amazing to realize that simply connecting with the source of all healing – heals. There is hope for everyone. There are effective methods for healing trauma in the mind and body today – that don't have to be costly, that don't have to take years and years of counseling, and that are easily repeatable so the person can do self-healing work on themselves. The SOS method is one.

It doesn't have to be complicated. My Intention is that one day soon, these forms of treatment will be readily accepted, so every person can find what will soothe their mind as simply as this. *I invite you to join me as the power of our combined Intention can shift this vision into reality more rapidly than we can even dream. Just imagine ...just imagine that.*

DARING LIFE TO
BE INCREDIBLE

I had no idea of the many profound and practical lessons I would learn as I voyaged into my new life. Phenomenal experiences had rocked my world in the past year; opening a timeless depth in Stillness of such riveting and wondrous magnitude that I knew I had been shown previews into the brilliance of our true potential. And while it was accelerating my awareness at warp speed, when lessons arrived to show the way, I often received them more begrudgingly than joyfully. At this point, the gut-wrenching lows were keeping pretty even with the spine-tingling highs.

I was going through a divorce, it was time to set up my new life, and with great determination I put an offer on a home. It was a complicated purchase, a building with many zoning issues that were over my head, but I had a vision of my new life, and when I walked into that spacious loft for the first time, I knew without a doubt it was exactly where I was supposed to be.

Important financial decisions were scary for me – my former husband had always handled the money. So, I hired a well-respected attorney to advise me in the many matters that I now had to handle on my own. I didn't listen to the initial warning signs going off in my head until I got a call from the owner's attorney informing me that I was about to lose the property because essential documents hadn't been turned over. The clock was ticking, and my time was about to run out. I was in a new world, swimming in a sea of fear.

My next wakeup came in the form of my attorney's invoice. I was being charged, in the first month, *double* what I had been advised I would pay for his entire services! *Poor divorced woman doesn't know what she's doing.* Is that what he thought? Could I have drawn this event into my life from those 'old tapes' playing in my head that *I wasn't smart enough?* Had those thoughts from my past been playing so loud, that I was now projecting it? Was I really so blind?

I politely asked the attorney why my timelines were about to be missed. It was then he chose to tell me that after reviewing everything closely, his advice was not to buy. I was speechless! I needed to make sense out of this situation, especially since I had discovered this *undesirable* property now had three backup offers just waiting for me to drop out! I'd hired this man to walk me through the rough terrain, to assist me in purchasing this safe haven, which would become my home. And now, through his brilliant counsel, I was in danger of losing it?! I felt so alone. Who could I turn to?

My inner knowing was about to teach me a big lesson. I had set an intention to find the best possible place for me to live. I had a vision of what it would look like, *and* when I found the property I knew it was my home. Somehow, I'd gotten blindsided by this man's credentials. Thinking he knew more than I did, I handed him the reins, and true to form, he was trying to take me for a ride.

Each time I followed the guidance from my newly expanded awareness, the rewards were off the charts. I had learned to set Intentions to guide me, and I had discovered where the field of potential opens that would ignite this possibility into my life. While I would bring in advisors to offer suggestions, it seemed my *knowing* always evidenced the best answers. All that I needed to do now was continue listening and allowing them in. When I tried to fully map out my life as I had before, with linear A, B, Cs of *I can make it happen,* the synchronicity would disappear. I was learning how to allow even greater plans to unfold by releasing my fears in the Stillness, and listening to what guidance revealed.

I got the message. I picked up the phone, called my attorney back, and fired him. Within 48 hours I became the happy owner of the building that everyone told me I shouldn't buy. The coming years revealed why this was the perfect decision to make.

Some of our habits and beliefs are so ingrained we don't even know we have them until an event appears to demonstrate where we are stuck. As strong as I seemed on the outside, I often took action from a place of fear. I had lived for years, thinking I wasn't smart enough because I had left home at 16 and only graduated with a GED, [2] (the equivalent of a High School Diploma). And, yet when I tapped into that highway of intelligence it consistently gave me better answers than those offered by my more educated advisors.

My new purchase was high on the list of contention. The reality was that top professionals *were* telling me this building would not be easy to manage, that I could lose all the money I had, and to just let it go. Their arguments were valid. The handbook I wanted that could tell me what to do was realized by consistently returning to the practices I had developed. I learned how to quiet the apprehension that would surface like a nauseating vice-grip squeezing my insides by taking walks while listening to Stillness Sessions, and by applying the tools that brought me answers of what to do. As the anxiety was released from my body, that loving, creative life force would send the inspiration I needed time and again.

I learned to let go of my pictures of not being smart enough, of not being as educated as I needed to be, as my knowing far surpassed any formal study I ever could have taken. The Intentions I set always guided me, and even though the journey wasn't easy, it taught me to trust implicitly. A core of strength I didn't know I had arrived like a gale-force wind out of nowhere with enduring intensity. Life became a symphony of sorts, where I learned to embrace challenges, knowing I was being guided each step of the way.

After three years that *knowing* told me it was time to move. The Intentions I had set, to find a new home, to find my new life's purpose, and to not feel so powerless became apparent through the extraordinary events that transpired. The developing neighborhood that I was warned would cause me catastrophic problems became the *it* locale. The building more than doubled in value. When I sold it there were seven backup offers, each valued at more than the last. People were mystified how something like this could happen.

As the building transformed, brick by brick, so did I, through tears and laughter, as old ways of being were replaced by the luminous power that resides in each one of us. It was a time I'll never forget – the ups, the downs, the highs and the lows. It wasn't always easy, but when you intend for the game of life to be the adventure it can be, then it becomes the truly incredible journey it is.

―――――

INSIGHTS, QUESTIONS & REFLECTIONS

Can ingrained patterns from the past really change? i.e. feeling powerless, not smart enough, etc? Each person has different emotional content – from transgenerational inheritance (*see Epigenetics, Part 3*) and from recent past events that are imprinted in the body-mind. As these blocks are released, a tendency to repeat the behavior lessens. What I find interesting in retrospect is that the challenges I faced inspired me to use the tools I had developed. So, it ultimately proved to be the perfect set of circumstances to go through – that not only diminished the anxiety I felt, but demonstrated how well the tools worked. Patterns from the past absolutely can change and will, depending on your application of these SOS Tools and connection to the advanced life Energy.

How long does it take? The length of time it takes to alter negative patterns depends on the presence of a harmonious energetic flow within the mind and body, which builds through application of the method. Some patterns completely release, you will even have a hard time remembering that you ever had them – and others hang on so you can learn from them as you chip away the blocks, like a sculptor revealing the beauty within the stone.

How long does it take for an Intention to become a reality? The Setting a Potent Intention Tool lists what gives your Intentions greater potency. Not all become reality if they are not in alignment with the best journey that brings you the knowing of your soul. There have been many twists and turns after connecting to higher awareness – some have been more challenging than others, but each one has given me greater strength and a deeper trust of the guidance I receive.

What can you do when it feels like events are demonstrating something totally different than what you intended? Become flexible. Look at what is missing. Reflect on these questions:

- Have my emotions been triggered? Do I want to keep losing my power every time something like this happens?
- Do I want outside influences to determine how I feel?
- Which SOS Tools can I use now to get new answers and get back on track?

Look and see if this could be the perfect time to Set a Potent Intention, and to amplify it with whichever audio format you are drawn to. You will find inspiration arriving so quickly. Ahhhh ... it's so nice to know where to go to get answers, isn't it?

Can limiting patterns be completely released? Many people who practice SOS tell me of patterns they had that are completely gone. And, there are layers of emotional content within each of us that can continue to release year after year. And, the promise of this book is that if you apply what you read here, many of your biggest challenges today will completely dissipate.

If something has come up for you while reading this, that you clearly want to let go of, I suggest *writing it down* now and then using it as a focus when doing the Release & Let Go Tool.

When you have deep experiences that give you new insight, do you immediately become in tune with all of life? Sometimes people think that when you have transcendent experiences you will never have another negative thought – it isn't like that. What happens is that you become aware of your limited thinking, of old patterns, which is wonderful as you now have the opportunity to release what isn't a part of the extraordinary light you truly are. And, you will find that negative tendencies have less and less of a hold on you, as more of your potential comes into the light of day.

SETTING POTENT INTENTIONS
why, when, what & how

As your Intention is sent into a quantum field of Energy, it has the organizing power to bring fulfillment. It creates a context for how you see yourself, what you want your life to be about, and what you believe is possible. If you are not bringing focused attention to your future through the inspiration you access from infinite intelligence you could be in *re*-action each day from whatever life presents. When you add the 'potency factor' to Intentions, you now add even more fuel to your vision.

Why is Setting Potent Intentions so impactful?
Adding the potency of the unified field resonating through Stillness Sessions Technology to the equation elevates the equation through *your* heightened vibration. It invites you to discover the power you have when you let your imagination play, release expectations and invite the adventure of life to unfold. Your Intentions have the ability to shape your life. They support circumstances to appear that are not only for long-term future fulfillment, but also participate in everyday life becoming more enjoyable. Events that you would like to see happen, such as job opportunities, travels to exciting places, reaching people you want to meet – and discovering new solutions when it feels like there aren't any – can bring possibilities you can't even dream.

When should I apply Setting Potent Intentions and what would change in my life by doing it regularly?

While your life can appear to be dictated by outer circumstances, what you realize by incorporating Setting Potent Intentions as a consistent practice is that you can shift that paradigm and completely transform your life experience. An Intention can spur a new idea into high gear; it can draw events, circumstances and people to you that benefit your life in numerous ways. Not every Intention will happen, and that's OK; remember you have invited the best possible guidance to bring you what is best for your evolutionary journey. And that is exactly what unfolds.

What is the difference between Intentions and goals?

Intentions aren't 'To Do' lists or goals, which have a sense of requiring effort to 'make it happen'. An Intention is an invitation to universal consciousness to create your future *with* you. There is less pressure and expectation, and more willingness for infinite guidance. Intentions have the power to set a direction or chart a course that inspires and generates your entire life.

It's important to look at how you feel about your Intention; if you are having internal fearful or depressed thoughts and emotions, they are broadcasting a frequency that diminishes your creative potential. Aligning your emotional content (conscious and unconscious) is essential to the overall impact you can have, and, it's not something you can fake. Which is why adding potency to your Intentions increases when limiting beliefs in the mind and body are released.

the diversity of your intentions

Intentions can be focused on how you want to use your talents and skills, relationships that you would like to have, both personal and in business. They can be for adventure and travel that invites an appreciation of nature, or just an overall passion for living, and to accelerate consciousness. Intentions can be focused in any of the following areas:

- Body
- Mind
- Spirit
- Career
- Travel
- Prosperity
- Relationships

SOS TOOL: SETTING POTENT INTENTIONS

1 APPLY TOOL & TEACHING:

a. **Explore**/review SOS Teaching

b. **Reflect with Three Breath Awareness** on one Intention that would assist you now – **short term**/one week – and one **long term**/three months+

c. **Write:** "My Intention is to …" (examples below)

- **Discover** _____ (greater prosperity, i.e. a career/job that matches my skills/what I value)
- **Develop** _____ (relationships that benefit my professional/personal life)
- **Become** more _____ (loving, fearless, compassionate)
- **Experience** greater _____ (peace of mind, joy, security)
- **Enjoy** _____ (vitality, mental and physical wellbeing)

2 ACTIVATE ENERGY POTENTIAL THROUGH STILLNESS SESSIONS TECHNOLOGY:

a. Listen to **Deep State Stillness** or an **Elevate Session**.

3 ACT ON INSPIRATION AS IT IS REVEALED:

a. Give yourself time to allow the Intentions to settle in, to dream and envision them, to unfold over time. Not all Intentions have immediate action points.

b. In the following week, **set action points** around the Intention you would like to bring into existence that has begun to appear. Follow through.

MORE EXAMPLES

Writing Intentions that draw an inspired future will bring events and circumstances that clarify why you want to consistently include Setting Potent Intentions in your life. It doesn't have to take long, less than 15 minutes to dream, design and activate your extraordinary life. I can't imagine time better spent – can you? Here are a few examples written by the SOS team:

1. I have a new career that matches my passion and brings greater prosperity.
2. I experience more peace of mind and release unneeded stress from my life.
3. Doors open and powerful relationships develop a magical future, where events unfold with ease and synchronicity.
4. Inspiration appears and world travel brings exquisite excitement, enthusiasm and joy to life.
5. I find the most loving person that is a match to my life, who is caring, kind and supportive.
6. I have a fabulously fun Friday filled with excitement and effortless synchronicity.
7. I overcome my fear of heights and become more courageous to ride roller coasters and climb mountains.
8. A new person joins our team that has tremendous skills as well as heart.
9. My body is healthy and filled with vitality, I find the perfect routine to support my journey. i.e. trainer, nutritionist, support group.

SPECIAL TIP: If the Intention doesn't become realized, it isn't time to fall into depression, or believe that you are not thinking *positively*. Instead, look to see where else you could be focused. Maybe this *shutdown* is actually guiding you toward something that could be more beneficial. Realizing the impact of applied intentionality can set visions into play that profoundly map out where your life will next lead you.

CONNECT

I have collected pictures, videos and audios of the people whose stories appear in this book I thought you might enjoy. You can check out the multi-media by clicking on the link or scanning the QR code:

www.theSOSmethod.com/sosconnect3

 Watch a video of Katie talking about being bullied at school

 Watch a video of Action Jackson talking about what happened that night on the plains of Africa

 Watch a video of Jeffrey talking about how he felt in the Stillness

begin as a mere apprentice

and the very power of love will lead you on

to become a master in the art

those who have made the most progress

will continually press on

never believing themselves

to have reached their end;

for charity should go on increasing

until we draw our last breath

Jean-Pierre Camus,
a French bishop, preacher and author

PART 6

THE SWEET
SPOT OF LIFE

DEEP PEACE & THE FLOW OF HIGHER CONSCIOUSNESS

There is a sweet spot of life that awaits each one of us. It is so delicious, so all encompassing, that it fuels love, contentment and joy into each day. Suffering is not a part of conscious living – it is a relic leftover from ancient doctrines that seemed to say, "misery makes you strong." Who told you that you have to suffer? It is actually more conscious to live in harmony with the flow of life, transmitting peace and awareness wherever you go.

I have seen hate transformed into love when a man in a state of unmitigated rage became caring and compassionate,[1] fear be replaced by inner strength and courage when women and men left abusive relationships they'd been in for years; self-defeating patterns be eliminated and replaced with a renewed passion for living. Momentous breakthroughs happen when you are connected with the advanced life Energy that brings love and inspiration into every day.

The remarkable events, qualities and circumstances that defined each person's life in this book are possible for you. They are not a distant dream, or something difficult to attain. In each story where people's lives continued to be filled with more joy, increased vitality, and the ability to find solutions to everyday challenges – the benefits occurred through cumulative practice of the SOS method. If you are wondering how you can *consistently* advance the love and potential in you – I think you will appreciate the simplicity of the various plans I developed. Finding what works for you that is flexible, fits your lifestyle, and is so enjoyable you look forward to it, will entice you to continually evolve. And isn't that what we all want.

IT'S JUST THE NEXT STEP

"That's one small step for man ... one giant leap for mankind."
Neil Armstrong's life-changing experience ignited these
words to be shared with the world. As he stepped onto the
moon – it inspired everyone watching to dream of what else
was possible – if something this remarkable could really
happen. How can you bring what you dream and all that you
envision into your life today?

the next giant leap for mankind

Sometimes the future can seem daunting, but when you
integrate the Energetic stream of intelligence, and envision
the future from the inspiration that arises – it's always *just
the next step*. In *Simply, Beautifully Powerful (see Part 5)*,
Betsy's inspiration revealed, "I never knew what I wanted
before; everything looked so big, so monumental. Now
it's easy for me to identify. Nothing's that big; *it's just the
next step*." She, like so many others who connected to that
exquisite power streaming through SOS, had taken a giant
leap into her future, and it wasn't challenging – it was
exciting. What is the next step for you?

Let me remind you again of your innate capabilities – *you
are a powerhouse of love and potential*. Developing a way to
consistently integrate the Energetic intelligence of life gives
you access to that creative power, peace and contentment that
is your birthright.

What we first must consider when looking at the next step is the model we have accepted for our education – if it is only based on cognitive learning, even computers will surpass our capabilities. The only way to foresee a future where humanity will not get left behind – is to access the inward, experiential journey that teaches us from the infinite intelligence we truly are.

good news ... bad news ... and the best news of all

So many people speak to me about complacency and how challenging it is to stay connected to what they value most. It's called the human condition. We all have it, that tendency to get swayed by outer activities that are so engaging we forget what is of greatest importance. There is also what occurs in the mind when chemical reactions have formed that literally magnetize addictive tendencies and negative events to be repeated, all confirming our identity of powerlessness (*see Neuroplasticity, Part 3*). Your choices, habits, behavior and resulting actions can create a life you love – or one that you often loathe.

It's not only the memories of your immediate past that cause your reaction to certain life situations, there is also the history of humanity's suffering that has entangled itself in the cells of your body. Blaming your childhood and your parents doesn't make sense when you realize they have some of the same epigenetic coding as you (*see Epigenetics, Part 3*), and they could have grown up in an environment where unconscious beliefs, even if well-intended, were implanted.

As research has shown us, the epigenetic Petri dish of life has been filled with traumatizing events since the beginning of time.[1]

staying open to discoveries of newfound power

While you are a powerhouse of potential, you could also be entrenched in a quicksand of genetic time. Discovering this doesn't have to be upsetting, it can actually be liberating when you take into consideration *The New Science (see Part 3),* combine it with what great wisdom teachings and ancient healing traditions have taught us, and realize what is possible now.

Ervin Laszlo, nominated twice for the Nobel Peace Prize, explains that, "In ages past, the connectedness and wholeness of the world was known to medicine men, priests, shamans, seers and sages, and to all people who had the courage to look beyond their nose and stay open to what they saw ..."[2] There is so much being revealed today that punctuates the importance of changing our outdated belief systems – the many doctrines stated as truth that don't support the recognition of our innate potential.

What you believe is a big part of the equation – *when you recognize you are not a victim of your DNA, your inheritance, or your mind*, what opens is a gateway to extraordinary new beginnings. And getting there – is *just* the next step.

Choices, Habits, Behavior & Actions
= Life Circumstances

We often look for ways to confirm the paradigms we already believe. When you free up your mind, you are given the power to alter your perspective. Acquiring new habits is not easy. But by rewiring the neural pathways that propagate negative patterns, you will not have to fight the mind to implement your Intentions. Your mind and body will become your friend, and will support your aspirations to become reality. Establishing empowered habits, behaviors and actions reveals the most extraordinary potential possible – and, it is up to you bring this shimmering possibility into the future.

from powerless to powerful

You may understand that taking better care of your body will make a difference in your life, but if you never exercise or go to the gym it could create a raft of mental, emotional and physical challenges; internal disappointment, ill health and further complacency. It also builds on the belief that you are powerless. Imagine how much unconsciousness and suffering would be released if everyone consistently connected to the Stillness within, and accessed that Energetic power of life.

Old beliefs might want to persist, but the light of absolute Love is so much more powerful. Connection to the inner peace that never leaves you continually expands the alchemy of true healing. The benefits you receive are directly proportionate to your ability to absorb and experience the information given – not just the words, but by connecting to this timeless dimension within you.

When you place yourself in a unified field of peace, your life begins to mirror what you experience. Your attachment for life to 'look a certain way' diminishes its control over you, and inspiration arises for life to be the precious and adventurous journey it is. Trust builds, courage appears, limiting beliefs dissolve and love grows. *Activating this power within you by using the SOS Tools and Technology, consistently incorporating it into every day* – brings remarkable coherence, the wholeness that highlights lasting transformation. Being extraordinary, accessing and living from your highest potential, is the next "giant leap for mankind" and, it's … just the next step.

tools for your evolutionary journey

Cumulative practice of SOS, in just minutes a day, brings phenomenal benefits that are life-lasting. Continuous cycling of these Tools will evidence how easily they become a part of your life – as conscious habits that bring enjoyment and support:

- Any time resistance arises, in any area of your life then: **Release & Let Go** will become your best friend.
- **Making Requests** will always bring greater knowledge and creative solutions to whatever you want to know.
- Accessing answers from intuitive knowing becomes a way of living, consciously accelerated by **Expanding Intuitive Abilities**. Life becomes more of an adventure than a chore.
- To transmit waves of healing consciousness through you, your thoughts and words, keep **Conscious Communication** as your guide.

• It's always the right time for **Setting Potent Intentions** to ignite your creative potential.

As you listen to Stillness Sessions you'll find that dynamic Energy within you elevating. By combining this profound technology with practical SOS Tools and Teachings, you'll receive continuous evidence of how the most difficult challenges can be transformed and the most exciting ideas can be realized. Releasing old patterns, developing new habits and behaviors and acquiring the ability to bring inspired actions into every day ignites that sweet spot of life.

To see massive transformation that continually develops *dynamic harmony and coherence*, it's always a good idea to implement a consistent plan. If you enjoy "putting on headphones and hitting play," the 21 Day Essentials Plan might be the best one for you.

Each day, month and year spent incorporating this cohesive method rapidly accelerates your connection with love, compassion, warmth and ingenuity, impacting your life and the lives of your family and friends, ultimately being transmitted out into the world.

This journey we are all on is a valuable treasure offered to each one of us as a gift. I invite you to celebrate with me, the timeless adventure that life is, and the friendship and unity our hearts recognize entwined in a future that we each can dream. Thank you for transforming this world by inviting the brilliance of you and your potential to shine through.

With Great Love,

Marlise

what greater loss
is there in life
than not to know
your very soul
what greater fear
is there to have

not of pain
not of loss
not of sadness
or change
but rather fear
the chains
that bind your mind

never tasting
never touching
never holding
never hearing
love's true call

Marlise Karlin

APPENDIX:
THE SCIENTIFIC STUDY OF THE SIMPLICITY OF STILLNESS METHOD
signposts that revolutionize the future – here and now

"I believe we are guided to pivotal moments so we can realize what is innate to all human beings – and what we have yet to fully recognize within ourselves. This knowing can shift the quality of your life beyond what might appear to be the meaningless circumstances that surround you.

"There were times in my life when the pain I lived with was unbearable, I don't know which was greater, the anger or the sadness. I remember thinking that I would do anything to change my situation, and yet I felt the ability to do this was completely out of my control. It wasn't. Years later as my life's journey evolved, I discovered just how misguided these beliefs were."

What do you say to people who are dealing with one of the most devastating illnesses on the planet today? I spoke these words not from knowing what it would be like to be in their position, but from what would be an even greater loss – never experiencing the Love that knows no boundaries, the peace that dissolves your suffering in a breath, and the Light that illumines every part of your life. Connecting to an experience of who you truly are – that, is what I do know.

And so began an eight-week odyssey I will never forget; the courageous people hidden behind masks of pain, the tears, the joy and the challenges. There were 26 people in the study, 19 with the motor-neuron disease amyotrophic lateral sclerosis (ALS) and seven caregivers. The people with ALS were at all different stages – from those who could still walk and take care of themselves to those who had to use voice boxes to speak.

I had been asked to develop a program for people with this disorder, which is commonly known as Lou Gehrig's disease; the damages to the neuromuscular system make it hard to walk, speak, eat, swallow and breathe. The majority of people with this condition only live 3–5 years although a few, like Stephen Hawking, the renowned theoretical physicist, have lived longer.

What can you offer someone who has literally been given a 'death sentence' to make them feel better? Are there really any words? It was easy to understand why, given their situation, many were in states of agitation, resignation and rage. Watching your life slip away – your ability to perform even basic necessities, like eating, walking and bathing, slowly being diminished day by day, must be incredibly frightening.

Only when a person's heart has been touched by the Love and power that exists there, can the mind begin to deal with complex circumstances like these. I have seen rage turn into pure love, as the healing Energy in SOS calms the mind, soothes the heat of emotional suffering, and ignites a uniquely different perception. I knew that bringing this experience into their lives was the first step. This is what the participants shared about how Stillness Sessions and the method affected them in the first two weeks (names have been changed for confidentiality):

It gives me a better frame of mind – like, I know I can handle this. – Kathryn, Caregiver

I am finding expansion in my breathing and emotions. Tears of relief happen frequently and some caregivers who are in the room while I play Stillness Sessions have also reported tears. –Darren, ALS

All day I was in a state of deep relaxation feeling more rejuvenated from that light that Marlise was speaking of. – Michael, ALS

I'm still in a sense of peace, relaxation. – Tara, Caregiver

It feels so nurturing, it seems to be countering the restrictiveness that I have found to be associated with ALS on every level. – Jeff, ALS

I feel very relaxed. All my overwhelming feelings are going away. – Joe, ALS

I have gone from hopelessness to hopefulness. – Susan, ALS

nothing stillness offers separates you
from your truth, by whatever name you give it

God (Protestant), Nature in its evolution, Energy, Spirit, Lord (Baptist), Jesus, Allah (Sufi), Source – these were all the names given by the participants in the study for what they believe makes this universe remain in motion. With this many differing points of view, it would be easy to imagine some might be challenged by the definition of Stillness or Energy, or any number of things, and yet, 96.5 percent confirmed an experience of greater peace and calm when listening to Stillness Sessions Technology.

When people are in this state of exquisite peace, everything that might normally separate them – religion, politics, financial differences – dissipates. Regardless of any belief system, what is inherent within all of us, where we find complete harmony and connection with each other is that experience of absolute love, pure peace.

My intention was to offer each person a way to deeply experience what exists beyond the physical. To give them the tools that bring a measurement of joy and the recognition of who they are beyond the body that no longer claims or supports them. I wanted them to know THAT, to experience THAT. This is what pulled me through the dark times when I was blinded by the pain of my past. In this well of peace, fear releases, you realize your inherent value, how very loved you are, then you can let go of the suffering and anguish that blame and anger cause. Once you get this, anything is possible.

the journey continues

While the method brought peace into their lives, there were also turbulent times as congested mental and emotional blocks appeared. When triggers from the past and painful memories surface that have been hidden in the unconscious, they often appear like a roaring lion, not willing to give up its territory. More than one of the participants with ALS would rage, as though it would signal to the powers that be that they would not be defeated.

Some of their stories were included in this book; people, just like you and me, going through what could be the most painful time in a human being's life, who found their light, and let it shine.

stunning breakthroughs ...
from struggle to hope

Over the course of the study, remarkable events occurred that challenged prevailing theories that mark the progression of emotional devastation when dealing with chronic illness. Families were able to communicate with each other in ways that set new markers for what is possible for us all. The improvement in the quality of people's lives in the study was significant. Here are just a few recorded experiences the participants reported, many in their own words:
* Recognition and release of past blocks and fears
* Acceptance and appreciation of self
* From anger to peace
* Feeling closer to God/ personal truth
* Finding value in life's small moments

- Experiencing deeper connection within
- Perspective on my life has shifted
- Don't have same worries as before
- A real sense of calmness
- Physical improvement in speaking
- Self-acceptance
- Interpersonal relationships have changed
- Loss of resistance

A couple of months after completion of the study, I was compiling my research papers from piles of transcripts when I received unfortunate news. It was discovered that there were certain procedural requirements not met, which would cause the findings to not be published. While this didn't affect what had been evidenced, it was certainly disappointing.

And, what was most important to me and why I did the study – was so that people who are looking for inner peace and the various mental, emotional and physical healing noted could experience what this method offers. When I think about the people I met, I am moved to tears. I am grateful for having the opportunity this scientific research on The Simplicity of Stillness Method offered; to observe what was possible in a structured manner, over an eight-week period, and to witness the loving awareness this Energy field ignites in a person's life in their most challenging hour.

The transcripts say it all, expressing what is often beyond rational understanding, to leave for the world signposts of how the conscious Awareness can revolutionize our future, beginning here and now.

The remarkable benefits people reported are possible for anyone going through a deeply troubled time. I trust those in need will find it through this book and through you. With great love I offer my gratitude to everyone who shared their lives.

INTENTION OF SCIENTIFIC STUDY

The intention of the study was to document the measurable effects of The Simplicity of Stillness Method in the improvement of quality of life, physical impairments, and psychological and social variables in the lives of people with ALS and caregivers.

CAREGIVERS

The study, initially for people with ALS, was expanded to include their caregivers – independently – as their frame of mind and health is vitally important to the wellbeing of the person they are caring for, as well as their own.

As is the case with most caregivers because of carrying the full weight of all financial and family responsibilities, many had time constraints and weren't able to attend. We were fortunate that those who joined could fully participate.

THE PROGRAM

People received the SOS Program digitally over an eight-week period. There were eight SOS Tools, written and in audio format. They also received three Stillness Session formats; Deep State Stillness, Sacred Word, and DNA Healing sound recordings. Email reminders of how the participants could integrate what they learned into the week ahead were sent bi-monthly.

Calls were made bi-monthly to both the people with ALS and the caregivers to supplement the lessons, invite questions, share their challenges, their 'wins', and their inspirational experiences with their group. Individual calls were provided at the completion of the study where each participant learned how to further integrate the SOS Method into their lives beyond the completion of the study. And to further record their insights, challenges and individual experiences that they might not have been able to report because of time constraints or privacy in the group calls.

LEARN MORE
To learn more about this program and others, how you can be a Simplicity of Stillness Facilitator, and to request it for your facility, foundation or hospital, contact info@marlisekarlin.com.

FACILITATING THE
SIMPLICITY OF STILLNESS

The purpose of all Simplicity of Stillness training is to support you to live from your highest potential and share that knowledge with others. In the SOS Facilitator Program you will learn the advanced tools of this scientifically researched method that rewire your brain and heal your body.

Facilitating is an extension of The SOS mission taught worldwide. The Simplicity of Stillness is facilitated in hospitals, rehabilitation and wellness centers and organizations working with at risk youth and people who suffer from various chronic illnesses.

SOS Facilitators can help people in large or small groups learn how to release mental, emotional and physical blocks, and access greater confidence, courage and clarity. The *Stillness Session Technology* can be taught to people who want to learn a rapid, direct form of meditation that releases stress and accelerates inspired opportunities.

SOS Facilitators are personally trained and certified by Marlise Karlin. If your heart's desire is to accelerate your own wellness journey and help others, you are invited to join this growing community.

To find out more about expanding your study and becoming an SOS Facilitator, go to www.theSOSmethod.com.

there is no better time

to look beyond the boundaries

of who you think you are

there is no better time

to be all you're destined to be

just beyond the dream

is a reality

your heart has been longing for

your inner knowing has the key

that opens every door

Marlise Karlin

I developed a 21 day plan that fits simply into your life just as it is right now. It is not only enjoyable and incredibly healing, it's effective. It impacts the quality of your life from the very first day – releasing stress and past trauma while enhancing your health, prosperity, and relationships.

I'm excited to share this process with you, as I know it can assist you to realize optimal wellbeing and happiness. To know more about this interactive and inspiring program just visit this link or QR code:

www.theSOSmethod.com

MAGNIFY vitality, creativity, and inspired solutions. Eliminate self-defeating patterns. The most comprehensive package.

EXPERIENCE soothing relief from stress, deep inner peace and advanced life energy. Calming, motivating and healing.

NOTES

The Long & Winding Road

1. Karlin, Marlise, "Preface" *The Power of Peace in You* (London, England: Watkins, 2012)

Activating Your Highest Potential

1. Hawkins, David R., *Healing and Recovery* (Sedona, Arizona: Veritas, 2009), p 52

New Avenues to Super-Awareness

1. "Taxi drivers' brains 'grow' on the job" (BBC News World Edition, March 2000) http://news.bbc.co.uk/2/hi/677048. stm

Ancient Art & The New Science

1. Jin Shin Jyutsu, *About Jin Shin Jyutsu*, "JIN SHIN JYUTSU is the Art of releasing tensions which are the causes for various symptoms in the body. https://www. jsjinc.net/pagedetails.php?id=jsj&ms=8."

2. Jin Shin Jyutsu, *About Mary*, "An Interview with Mary Burmeister, Master of Jin Shin Jyutsu" https://www.jsjinc. net/pagedetails.php?id=about-mary&ms=8

3. Lipton, Bruce, interview by Marlise Karlin, November 5, 2013. See first CONNECT page.

Notes

Energy & Awareness

1. Tiller, William A, interview by Marlise Karlin, August 16, 2012. See first CONNECT page.
2. Siddha Yoga, *The Texts of Vedanta* "Vedanta, which emphasizes the one supreme principle that is the foundation of the universe." http://www.siddhayoga.org/teachings/vedanta
3. Jin Shin Jyutsu, *Welcome* "physio-philosophy is an ancient art harmonizing life energy in the body." https://www.jsjinc.net/
4. Sheldrake, Rupert, *Morphic Resonance* (Rochester, Vermont: Inner Traditions International, 2009)
5. Laszlo, Ervin, *Science and the Reenchantment of the Cosmos* (Rochester, Vermont: Inner Traditions, 2006)
6. Hawkins, David R., MD, PhD, *Power vs. Force: The Hidden Determinants of Human Behavior* (United States: Hay House, Inc., 1995, 1998, 2002), p 132

The Elements

1. Davis, Wade, *The Wayfinders* (Toronto, Ontario: Anansi Press, 2009)

Epigenetics

1. Venter, J. Craig, *Life at the Speed of Light* (New York: Viking Adult, 2013)
2. Lipton, Bruce, interview by Marlise Karlin, November 5, 2013. See third CONNECT page.

3. Pembrey, Marcus, and Bygren, Lars Olov, *Ghost in Your Genes*, PBS: NOVA, October 16, 2007

4. Seckl, Jonathan, *The Ghost in Your Genes*, BBC: Horizon, 2005.

5. Yehuda, Rachel, et. al., "Transgenerational Effects of Posttraumatic Stress Disorder in Babies of Mothers Exposed to the World Trade Center Attacks during Pregnancy" (*The Journal of Clinical Endocrinology & Metabolism*, July 2005)

6. Semmelweis Society International, *Dr. Semmelweis Biography* "Semmelweis is considered a pioneer of antiseptic procedures." http://semmelweis.org/about/dr-semmelweis-biography/

DNA

1. Hurley, Dan, "Grandma's Experiences Leave a Mark on Your Genes" (*Discover Magazine*, May 2013) http://discovermagazine.com/2013/may/13-grandmas-experiences-leave-epigenetic-mark-on-your-genes

2. "The Language of DNA: Can DNA Be Reprogrammed by Words and Frequencies?" (The Noetic Digest, October 2011). http://noeticdigest.wordpress.com/2011/10/11/the-language-of-dna-can-dna-be-reprogrammed-by-words-and-frequencies

3. Sagan, Carl "Life", *Encyclopedia Britannica Macropaedia* (1974), p 893-894.

4. Fosar, Grazyna and Bludorf, Franz, *Vernetzte Intelligenz* (Omega-Verlag: Dusseldorf, 2001)

5. Dyer, Wayne, *There's a Spiritual Solution to Every Problem* (New York: Harper Collins, 1975)

6. Hunt, Valery V., *Infinite Mind: Science of the Human Vibrations of Consciousness* (Malibu Publishing, 1996)

7. Hawkins, David R., *Relativity and Subjectivity* (Sedona, Arizona: Veritas, 2003), p 133

Brain Power

1. "Taxi drivers' brains 'grow' on the job" (BBC News World Edition, March 2000) http://news.bbc.co.uk/2/hi/677048.stm

2. King, Larry, *Change Your Mind, Change Your Life*, CNN: Larry King Live, August 2008

3. Bolte Taylor, Jill, PhD, *My Stroke of Insight* (New York: The Penguin Group, 2006)

4. Daggett, Willard R., Ed.D. and Nussbaum, Paul David, Ph.D., *How Brain Research Relates to Rigor, Relevance and Relationships* (International Center for Leadership in Education) http://www.leadered.com/pdf/How_Brain_Research_Relates_to_RRR_2014.pdf

5. Sapolsky, Dr. Robert, *Stress Portrait of a Killer*, National Geographic Special, September 23, 2008 http://killerstress.stanford.edu/

6. Buzsaki, Gyorgy, *Rhythms of the Brain* (New York: Oxford University Press, 2006)

7. Karlin, Marlise, "From Depression to Elation", *The Power of Peace in You* (London, England: Watkins, 2012)

Sound, Subtle Energies & Stillness Sessions

1. Hawkins, David, *Power vs. Force* (Sedona, Arizona: Veritas, 1995).
2. Tiller, William A., *Science and Human Transformation: Subtle Energies, Intentionality and Consciousness* (Walnut Creek, California: Pavior Publishing, 1997).
3. Science Learning, *Fundamentals of Waves* "Every wave has a specific wavelength" http://www.sciencelearn.org.nz/Science-Stories/Tsunamis-and-Surf/Fundamentals-of-waves
4. Massachusetts Institute of Technology, *Tuning Forks: Resonance & Beat Frequency:* "Striking one tuning fork will cause the other to resonate at the same frequency." http://video.mit.edu/watch/tuning-forks-resonance-a-beat-frequency-11447/

Defining New Horizons

1. Karlin, Marlise, "Man Who Would be Monk" *The Power of Peace in You* (London, England: Watkins, 2012)
2. Ibid.

Death & Dying, From Fear To Love

1. Emoto, Dr. Masaru, *What is the Photograph of the Frozen Water Crystals:* "The result was that we always observed beautiful crystals after giving good words, playing good music, and showing, playing, or offering pure prayer to water. On the other hand, we observed disfigured crystals in the opposite situation." http://www.masaru-emoto.net/english/water-crystal.html

Powerless to Powerful

1. Mate, Gabor, M.D. & Levine, Peter, Ph.D, "Appendix 3: The Prevention of Addiction", *In the Realm of Hungry Ghosts* (Berkeley, California: North Atlantic Books, 2011)

Training the Brain

1. Pecci, Dr. Ernest F., M.D. "Foreword", *Science and Human Transformation: Subtle Energies, Intentionality and Consciousness* (Walnut Creek, California: Pavior Publishing, 1997)

One Man's Cry for Love

1. The Lesson in the SOS Scientific Study was similar to the SOS ToolKit on Forgiveness www.marlisekarlin.com

Letting Go of What You Don't Want to Get What You Do

1. Advaita Yoga Ashrama, *Kundalini Yoga* http://yoga108. org/pages/show/94-kundalini-yoga-introduction-to-the-basic-concepts-of-kundalini-yoga

What You Don't Know Can Hurt You

1. A social anxiety disorder documentary: *Afraid of People* (American Public Television, 2002) http://www.youtube. com/watch?v=gmEJEfy5f50

2. Kagan, Jerome, "Temperament and the Reactions to Unfamiliarity" *Child Development Vol. 68, No. 1* (Blackwell Publishing, 1997) pp 139–143

Notes

3. Jin Shin Jyutsu, *About Mary*, "An Interview with Mary Burmeister, Master of Jin Shin Jyutsu" https://www.jsjinc. net/pagedetails.php?id=about-mary&ms=8

Wordless Insights

1. Hawkins, David "A Map of Consciousness" *Healing and Recovery* (Sedona, Arizona: Veritas, 2009)
2. Mate, Gabor, M.D. & Levine, Peter, Ph.D, "The Keys of Paradise", *In the Realm of Hungry Ghosts* (Berkeley, California: North Atlantic Books, 2011)

The Ultimate Brilliance: Inner & Outer Knowledge

1. Tiller, William A., interview by Marlise Karlin, August 16, 2012. See first CONNECT page.
2. Buzsaki, Gyorgy, *Rhythms of the Brain* (New York: Oxford University Press, 2006)

Your Intuitive Intelligence

1. Karlin, Marlise, "Listening to the Messages", *The Power of Peace in You* (London, England: Watkins, 2012)

Flights of Hope and Promise

1. Jackson, Action, interview by Marlise Karlin, October 13, 2010. https://www.youtube.com/watch?v=17E674Bo40A

Thinking, Speaking & Transmitting

1. Tiller, William A., interview by Marlise Karlin, August 16, 2012. See first CONNECT page.
2. Hawkins, David, *Healing and Recovery* (Sedona,

Arizona: Veritas, 2009) p 52

3. Smithsonian, *There are 37.2 Trillion Cells in Your Body* http://www.smithsonianmag.com/smart-news/there-are-372-trillion-cells-in-your-body-4941473/?no-ist

4. USGS Water Science School, *The water in you* http://water.usgs.gov/edu/propertyyou.html

5. Karlin, Marlise, "Prelude" *The Power of Peace in You* (London, England: Watkins, 2012)

6. Hawkins, David, *Power vs. Force* (Sedona, Arizona: Veritas, 1995).

7. Tiller, William A., *Psychoenergetic Science: A Second Copernican-Scale Revolution* (Walnut Creek, California: Pavior, 2007)

Super-cool ... Selena's New Life

1. Lipton, Bruce, *Spontaneous Evolution* (Carlsbad, California: Hay House, 2010)

Rock n Roll, Drugs & Higher Learning

1. Massachusetts Institute of Technology, *Tuning Forks: Resonance & Beat Frequency:* "Striking one tuning fork will cause the other to resonate at the same frequency" http://video.mit.edu/watch/tuning-forks-resonance-a-beat-frequency-11447/

2. Mate, Gabor, M.D. & Levine, Peter, Ph.D, *In the Realm of Hungry Ghosts* (Berkeley, California: North Atlantic Books, 2011) p 331

Transmitting Conscious Communication

1. Tiller, William A., interview by Marlise Karlin, August 16, 2012. See first CONNECT page.

Adding Potency to Highly Focused Thoughts

1. Covey, Stephen, *The 7 Habits of Highly Effective People* (Salt Lake City, Utah: FraklinCovey Co, 1989)
2. Tesla, Nicola, circa 1942
3. Tiller, William A., interview by Marlise Karlin, August 16, 2012. See first CONNECT page.
4. Tiller, William A., interview by Marlise Karlin, *Psychoenergetic Science: A Second Copernican-Scale Revolution* (Walnut Creek, California: Pavior, 2007)

The Relentless Pain of Being a Hero

1. Karlin, Marlise, *The Power of Peace in You* (London, England: Watkins, 2012)
2. Jin Shin Jyutsu, *About Mary*, "An Interview with Mary Burmeister, Master of Jin Shin Jyutsu" https://www.jsjinc.net/pagedetails.php?id=about-mary&ms=8
3. CNN, *The Uncounted* "22 veterans kill themselves every day" http://www.cnn.com/interactive/2014/03/us/uncounted-suicides/

Deep Peace & the Flow of Higher Consciousness

1. Karlin, Marlise, "The Angry Man", *The Power of Peace in You* (London, England: Watkins, 2012)

It's Just the Next Step

1. Hurley, Dan, "Grandma's Experiences Leave a Mark on Your Genes" (*Discover Magazine*, May 2013) http://discovermagazine.com/2013/may/13-grandmas-experiences-leave-epigenetic-mark-on-your-genes

2. Laszlo, Ervin, *Science and the Reenchantment of the Cosmos* (Rochester, Vermont: Inner Traditions, 2006)

ARTISTIC CREDITS

Thank you so much to the artists for creating exquisite visuals that invite our senses to engage in even deeper understanding of the journey revealed.

1. *Sight* Image Copyright gst, 2014. Used under license from Shutterstock.com.

2. *Sound* Image Copyright agsandrew, 2014. Used under license from Shutterstock.com.

3. *Touch* Image Copyright WonderfulPixel, 2014. Used under license from Shutterstock.com.

4. *Intention* Image Copyright ClickHere, 2014. Used under license from Shutterstock.com.

5. Numbers *1, 2, and 3* Images Copyright Sarawut Aiemsinsuk, 2014. Used under license from Shutterstock.com.

6. *Brain* Image Copyright Fedorov Oleksiy, 2014. Used under license from Shutterstock.com.

Notes

7. *Body* Image Copyright Robert Gonchar Vlad and Sebastian Kaulitzki, 2014. Used under license from Shutterstock.com.

8. *Spirit* Image Copyright amudsen, 2014. Used under license from Shutterstock.com.

9. *Audio, Video and PDF* Images Copyright punsayaporn, 2014. Used under license from Shutterstock.com.

10. *Deep State* Image Copyright Bogdan Tymofiienko, 2014. Used under license from Shutterstock.com.

11. *Elevate* Image Copyright khz, 2014. Used under license from Shutterstock.com.

12. *Sacred Word* Image Copyright Teguh Mujiono, 2014. Used under license from Shutterstock.com.

ADDITIONAL RESOURCES

– Karen Elkins www.sciencetosage.com
– Elliot Maynard www.arcoscielos.com
– Ron Willingham www.authenticsalesperson.com

ACKNOWLEGDMENTS

When I think of how perfectly my life has come together, the ups *and* the downs; the golden threads of people and events that arrived at the perfect time – I am deeply grateful. I could not be who I am today, if you weren't who you are. It is the love, support, insight and generosity of spirit that each of you has given me that inspired this book and my life.

I am fortunate to have been touched by the genius of Bill Tiller, Ph.D. who continues to light up my world with his wisdom, warmth and kindness, and by Jean, his wife, who demonstrates how heart, intuitive knowing and irreverence can joyfully coexist. Thank you to all scientists and doctors, which include Bruce Lipton, Ph.D. and Dr. Gabor Mate, who stem the tides of resistance, bravely leading others into innovative and compassionate new worlds.

To Mary Burmeister for your constant loving guidance, and to David Burmeister for carrying the torch forward so many can share in the exquisite teachings of Jin Shin Jyutsu. My gratitude to all doctors, and especially Dr. Susan Jamieson, who developed inroads to wellness that break down paradigms of *only my way* kind of thinking.

Those who stand, often in the shadows, without whom I would not be so consistently motivated – you have my heartfelt thanks and gratitude; Michelle Britzius, who keeps the ship running, Joe Pena, whose attentive listening brings the best answers, Gail Torr, who knows how to create magic, and Susan Mears, whose smiling countenance steers the often rough waters. A special thank you to Jo Lal, my publisher and Dawn Bates for your assistance in bringing SOS 3 to greater simplicity and clarity. To all the people whose stories appear here, your courage and strength inspire me, thank you for sharing your life.

And to You who draws the illumined knowledge of remembrance that ignites a future beyond dreams – I love you. May people everywhere heal, connect and experience that liquid Love you so freely share.

DOWNLOADING & MORE

This book includes Stillness Sessions Technology in three formats. You can receive them immediately by:

- Going to the **"Just For You – Stillness Sessions"** page at the front of the book or at the end of *Part 4: Stillness Sessions*.
- Copying the link on the page into your browser on your computer, tablet or smart phone or scan the QR code.This sends you to a page on the Simplicity of Stillness website for downloads or CDs.
  - **Downloads:** there are directions on how to download and begin listening instantly.
  - **Physical CDs:** there are also instructions of how to order a CD by mail.

Suggestion: Place the Stillness Sessions in several locations to make them easy to access: cell phone, mp3 device, iPad, Kindle, tablet, computer, etc.

Friends & Family: Listening to the Stillness Sessions is elemental for having the experiences and benefits you read about in this book. If you need assistance downloading ask a friend or family member for help and then enjoy listening with them, or ...

Contact us: If there is any way we can assist you, please contact us at customercare@marlisekarlin.com

WATKINS

Sharing Wisdom Since
1893

The story of Watkins Publishing dates back to March 1893, when John M. Watkins, a scholar of esotericism, overheard his friend and teacher Madame Blavatsky lamenting the fact that there was nowhere in London to buy books on mysticism, occultism or metaphysics. At that moment Watkins was born, soon to become the home of many of the leading lights of spiritual literature, including Carl Jung, Rudolf Steiner, Alice Bailey and Chögyam Trungpa.

Today our passion for vigorous questioning remains resolute. With over 350 titles on our list, Watkins Publishing continues to be at the cutting edge. Our books reflect the development of spiritual thinking and new science over the past 120 years, and we stay committed to publishing titles that change lives.

DISCOVER MORE...

Read our blog

Watch and listen to
our authors in action

Sign up to our
mailing list

JOIN IN THE CONVERSATION

f WatkinsPublishing   @watkinswisdom

WatkinsPublishingLtd   +watkinspublishing1893

Our books celebrate conscious, passionate, wise and happy living.
Be part of the community by visiting

www.watkinspublishing.com